Richard ...

Chieftain

Britain's Flawed Masterpiece

FV 4201 Chieftain Main Battle Tank

Published in Poland in 2019
by STRATUS s.j.
Po. Box 123,
27-600 Sandomierz 1, Poland
e-mail: office@mmpbooks.biz
as
MMPBooks,
e-mail: rogerw@mmpbooks.biz
© 2019 MMPBooks.
http://www.mmpbooks.biz

ISBN
978-83-65958-29-7

Editor in chief
Roger Wallsgrove

Editorial Team
Bartłomiej Belcarz
Robert Pęczkowski
Artur Juszczak

Colour profiles
JP Vieira

Scale Plans
Dariusz Karnas

Proofreading
Roger Wallsgrove

DTP
Stratus sp. j.

Printed by
Wydawnictwo
Diecezjalne i Drukarnia
w Sandomierzu
www.wds.pl

PRINTED IN POLAND

Table of contents

Acknowledgements

I would first like to thank my fellow Mushroom Author, Mr Phil Cater, as without his constant encouragement, and support in sub-editing and advising on the production process, this book would never have been completed. Cheers Phil!

I would also like to thank all the ex-Chieftain crew, former members of 1 RTR, REME and others who have allowed me to retell their stories, or use their photographs in this book.

Richard Kent

Chapter One

From Paper to Prototypes

Serious design studies for what would become the Chieftain began in 1950, under the title Medium Tank No. 2. The original proposal for a future Centurion replacement had been made in 1946 as the "Universal Tank" concept. With the Second World War not long over, and the Centurion proving to be the best Western tank of the era, the Universal Tank was considered an unaffordable luxury, so was quietly forgotten. By the early 1950s, the Ministry of Supply could see that Centurion, while a superb and flexible design, was reaching the end of its development potential. It would inevitably be matched by the newer generation of Russian armour, likely to becoming completely outclassed by the mid-1960s.

While some design studies had begun in 1950, it was not until 1953, when a report on the future of the tank in the British Army was commissioned from FVRDE (Fighting Vehicles Research and Development Establishment), that serious work began. In the autumn of 1953, HM Treasury reluctantly

Chieftain concept model. Very different to the actual production vehicle. (Crown Copyright)

The AMX 13 with its oscillating turret was technically impressive but the tactical doctrine it was built to serve was fundamentally flawed and resulted in many unnecessary deaths.

gave provisional approval for development funding. On 15th March 1954, a Policy Statement on the new Medium Gun Tank was released, marking the official birth of what was to become Chieftain.

In a moment of uncommon clarity and decisiveness, it was decided to dust off and update the Universal Tank Concept, taking into account the reality of the Cold War, and the financial constraints likely to be placed on development by successive Governments. Unusually, given the conservative nature of the Army establishment, the engineers and designers were encouraged to give their imaginations free rein – what might today be called an exercise in 'blue sky thinking', which produced various concepts, some of which were researched extensively, others quickly discarded.

One of the first ideas to be looked at was the one-man tank – the rationale being that if a tank with a four-man crew was good, then four one-man tanks were better, and this could offer some parity against the overwhelming Soviet superiority in numbers. The reality of the workload for a single crewman ended that project.

Paired two-man vehicles of around fifteen tons were looked at on paper – one armed with a recoilless rifle or High Velocity Gun (HVG), the other with guided missiles. Logistical considerations and the tactical inflexibility of the concept killed that idea.

Next came the coupled vehicle, with a heavily armoured fighting compartment and lightly armoured automotive element. This offered significantly enhanced mobility, and the option of in-service upgrades replacing one or the other part of the coupled unit. But the inherent complexity of the design, and its inferior all round visibility (unless the gun was mounted high on a tower structure) meant this proposal was discarded.

A turret-less fixed gun (similar to the Swedish S-Tank) was briefly considered, but was again discarded, due to the lack of tactical flexibility in the design. A turret-less tank cannot fire on the move, cannot protect or engage targets except in its frontal arc, and the gun cannot even be roughly aimed, until the vehicle stops. It has inherently poor cross-country performance, due to the short length of track in contact with the ground. (If the track run is long enough to give a comfortable ride cross-country, then it is too long to allow acceptable elevation, and if short enough to allow adequate elevation – it's too short for an acceptable ride). This turret-less tank concept should not be confused with the so-called "JagdChieftain" Concept Test Rig, which came much later, outlined in the Specialised Variants chapter of this book.

Project *Prodigal*

No account of Chieftain development would be complete without mentioning the one concept that almost made it to service, or at the very least, prototype stage – the almost mythical Project *Prodigal*. This evolved from the one-man tank proposal, it being realised that a small air-portable tank would be a useful asset in the low intensity conflicts and police actions popping up all over the last vestiges of Empire.

Development of this offshoot from the Future MBT programme, as Chieftain was known by then, was given the go-ahead in 1960. The original design looks like something out of a *Terminator* movie, with twin 120 mm recoilless rifles mounted above a low wedge-shaped tracked chassis, fed by two seven round drum magazines mounted on each side and above the vehicle. When crew fatigue and maintenance demands were considered, this configuration was abandoned, and the vehicle design repeatedly changed over the lifetime of the project.

The final incarnation of Project *Prodigal* had evolved into an open-topped two-man tracked vehicle, with a standard High Velocity gun in a fixed mount along the centreline. There are persistent rumours that at least three prototypes of the changing variants of this vehicle were built, but no records or photographs have ever been found – although some claim the FV 4401 Contentious prototype held in the Bovington Tank Museum Reserve Collection is one of the fabled vehicles, which does closely match the final paper design. Project *Prodigal* might have failed, but the air portable lightweight tank concept was finally realised in the successful CVR(T) (Scorpion/Scimitar) family.

THREE-QUARTERS FRONT VIEW NEARSIDE

A very rare picture of the original Project Prodigal with twin 120 mm recoiless rifles. (Crown Copyright)

FV 4401 Contentious at Bovington (Simon Q, via Wikimedia Commons)

Mock up of Project Prodigal in its second incarnation. (Crown Copyright)

A conventional tank with an oscillating turret was also given far more consideration than it warranted – perhaps solving the technical challenges involved appealed to the designers. This is a system which raises the entire turret to gain elevation for the gun, sections of armour concertinaed into each other to rise up and down with the turret. Eventually, practicality won out, as the overlapping armour filled the fighting compartment, and proved impossible to seal against NBC (Nuclear Biological Chemical) intrusion. The French AMX 13 designers overcame these problems simply by ignoring the NBC threat, and having the tank very lightly armoured, designed around the *"shoot and scoot"* theory. This French-championed idea was shown to be fatally flawed, and in reality meant the enemy shooting the tank full of holes while it attempted to scoot – less *"shoot and scoot"*, more turkey shoot. A deficient design and concept, which led to the deaths of many Israeli AMX 13 tank crews in the Six Day War.

To allow the largest gun possible to be fitted, a cleft turret was given serious consideration. This concept split the turret crew, requiring a semi-automatic loader but allowing the gun unlimited recoil, so removing the problems of fume extraction and empty shell casings littering the turret floor, but the additional weight and height compared to a conventional turret proved impractical.

Several more weird and wonderful designs were conjured up before it was accepted that a conventional "three box" tank was the best solution to the design brief that had been issued.

These exhaustive initial research and design studies were completed and submitted to the oversight committee for all new AFV designs. This was the Concepts Design Group, led by the its Principal Engineer, Leslie Monger. It was clear that none would provide a better basic platform than a conventional tank with a revolving turret, mounting a large calibre high velocity gun, and so this became the framework for the proposed Centurion replacement.

The Concepts Design Group, co-ordinating the various specialist design teams from FVRDE, ARDE (Armament Research and Development Establishment), Royal Ordnance Factory (ROF) Leeds, Leyland and Vickers-Armstrongs at Newcastle, to name but a few of the establishments and companies involved, had to consider many factors. These included the likely prevailing battlefield conditions and political constraints influencing the future British tank, outlined in various GSRs (General Staff Requirements) incorporating these into the new vehicle – the most important aspects being:

- The new tank would always face far greater numbers.
- It would almost always be fighting from a defensive position.
- Crew protection was paramount, tank crews being a highly skilled, limited and expensively trained resource.
- The main armament had to be capable of defeating current and future generations of Soviet armour – before their weapons came into range.
- The vehicle needed to be agile – *not fast* – and its mobility had to be *at least* as good as Centurion's.

- It needed NBC protection – as the future battlefield was expected to be awash with the effects of such weapons.
- Weight was to be limited to 45 tons, to avoid having to design deep wading gear and be able to use existing bridges.
- The need to future-proof the new vehicle as much as possible, as it would have to have a service life of at least twenty years, due to budgetary constraints.

Horstmann suspension unit with evil spring in situ. (RK)

The radical thinking of the early concepts was carried over into what at first appeared to be a conventional three-box design – driver front, turret middle and engine rear – but was in fact full of innovative ideas and developments – some good, others less so.

Tank design has to juggle three fundamental elements – Firepower, Armour protection and Mobility – the so-called *Holy Trinity*. Each country had its own ideas as to which of these took precedence. The British had been deeply affected by the horrific losses suffered by tank crews in WWII, due to weak armour, dangerous ammunition stowage and inadequate armament, so in the new tank, design priority was given to firepower, with armour protection a close second, and mobility a distant third. Once these priorities had been decided, serious work began in 1956 on finalising the design of what had become known as the Future Main Battle Tank (FMBT).

Leyland Motors were appointed as the main design contractors for the now officially designated FV 4201, but they were fully occupied with producing the Centurion Mk 7/8, and progress was initially slow. They did, however, build three proof of concept vehicles – the so-called 40 Ton Centurions, using Centurion automotive and running gear components. These highly classified machines were designed to test the recumbent driver's position, and the lack of an external mantlet for the gun. The radical decision to do away with an external mantlet was taken to prevent a "firepower kill", where a hit on the mantlet could jam the main armament or damage the trunnions, rendering the tank useless. This also allowed for the ideal ballistic shape of turret to be incorporated into the construction of the Chieftain. This omitted feature was concealed behind a canvas cover on the Centurion testbeds and Chieftain prototypes.

Two of the three 40 Ton Centurions are known to have survived. One is at the Bovington Tank Museum Reserve Collection; the other was at REME Borden – though the current location of this vehicle is unknown. As for the third, there are claims it was sent by mistake to Israel with a batch of Centurions, but its ultimate fate is also unknown. Perhaps it found good use in subsequent development of the Merkava 1's very similar gun mounting and recumbent driver positions. Or maybe it never made it to Israel – as Bovington has had a 40 Ton Centurion turret on display (in the overspill car park) for many years.

The recumbent driver's position when closed down was developed to keep the tank's silhouette as low as possible. The distinctive sloping front of the Chieftain was intended to give the best ballistic

shape to the frontal armour. The kink at the front of the cast plate was introduced at the last minute, to allow for taller drivers to fit in the cab. It would have made more sense to limit the height of the driver, as the Russians were known to do on their tank designs.

Initially, a welded front hull was considered, but it was decided to take advantage of the skills of British steelworkers to create a single casting for the hull front, thus providing greater strength and resistance to penetration. It is one of the many myths of Chieftain development that the sloping cast front was decided upon when a Soviet IS-2 tank (which has this feature) was discovered buried under a collapsed building in the British sector of Berlin. Great lengths were taken to keep the shape of the hull front secret during the development and trial period. Photos of the prototype and Mk 1 vehicles show this area covered by a large box structure, incorporating the headlights. *(Note for modellers – this obviously fooled Tamiya, as their 1/25ʰ Chieftain is moulded with the false front!)*

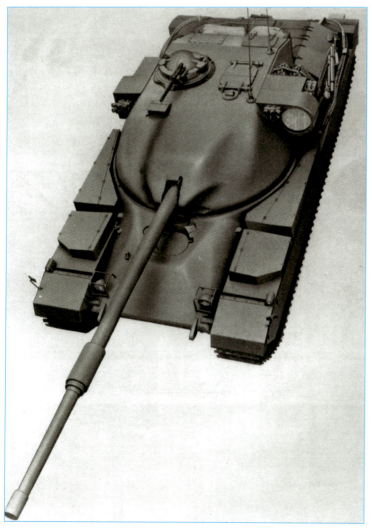

Various suspension configurations were considered by Leyland and then discarded, such as torsion bars (made the tank too tall), and hydrogas (too immature a technology at this point). So it is no real surprise, given Leyland's familiarity with these units, that an improved version of the Centurion's Horstmann suspension units was settled upon. Horstmann suspension is a developed form of 'Horizontal Volute Spring Suspension', in which the individual units are bolted to the side of the tank, hypothetically allowing easy replacement in the field, if damaged by a mine. The suspension, while not perfect, gave good cross-country performance, much superior to the Leopard 1. Chieftain was able to maintain a higher tempo of cross-country speed and for much longer periods than Leopard 1, which was fast on roads, but forced crews to slow down cross-country, due to its punishing ride characteristics.

The hull design was progressing well, and it was intended that the new tank would have a V8 Rolls-Royce diesel engine… when, for reasons never adequately explained, a decision was taken to adopt a multi-fuel powerplant, in line with the recommendation of the NATO Standardisation Committee, that all future NATO vehicles should have such engines. The saga of the L60 engine was a shameful episode in the history of British tank design – a book could be written on that subject alone. In fact, several scathing reports were written for MOD and Government, which can now be accessed by the interested public. Here, the whole sorry tale has been summarised in a later chapter of this book – for those who can bear to read it.

Compared to the hull and automotive problems, development of the turret and main armament proceeded smoothly, for the most part. It had been decided at an early stage that the main armament needed to defeat 120 mm of armour, sloped at 60 degrees, and at a range of 1.8 km (1.1 miles). Scientists at FVRDE and ARDE came to the conclusion that a calibre of 120 mm was best suited for such a gun. As it was also required to fire HESH (High Explosive Squash Head) rounds, a rifled barrel was specified, as opposed to the smoothbore preferred by other nations.

The large calibre of the gun gave designers three main problems, all related to ammunition – size, stowage and

The bag charge bins were fitted below the turret ring low in the hull for extra safety, and filled with pressurised antifreeze which would flood the charge to contain or extinguish a fire in the unlikely event that a bin was penetrated. (RK)

Good comparison of the height and widths of Conqueror, Centurion and Prototype Chieftain. (Crown Copyright)

A Chieftain Mk 1 demonstrating its hill climbing ability. Note the flat 3 deck early transmission covers, rudimentary NBC system and integrated one piece rear bins. (Crown Copyright)

weight. Traditionally, a brass case contains the propellant, with the projectile fixed on top, which in the case of a 120 mm round, means it is tall, bulky and extremely heavy – approximately 50 kgs (110 lbs). The turret would also have to be very large, to allow room for the loading of the shell. Experience with the Conqueror heavy tank showed that a loader could not maintain the required rate of fire, due to fatigue. A loading trial with the Conqueror heavy tank showed that a loader could maintain the required rate of fire over the span of a single engagement (up to 25 rounds) but he could not load fast enough to meet the requirement for six rounds in the first minute, and the rate of fire steadily dropped, the longer the engagement. Nor could an adequate ammunition load be carried, due to lack of stowage space.

In trying to solve these problems, many different options were considered, such as a liquid propellant gun, on which vast amounts of time and money were expended, to no avail. The liquid propellant gun remains the Holy Grail of gun designers, but none have ever made it into service. An autoloader was also considered. Again, the size and complexity, and potential for reliability issues, coupled with a low rate of fire, plus the increased maintenance load on a reduced crew, quickly saw that proposal dropped. Autoloading systems have since been shown to have a significant risk of a turret hit causing a chain firing of the ammunition in the carousel – something Russian tanks appear very prone to.

At some point, one of the design team came up with the idea of multi-part ammunition, the so-called bag charge concept. This is often referred to as two-part ammunition, but is in fact made up of three parts – the projectile, the bag charge, and the vent tube, which ignites the bag charge. This was not exactly a new idea, as the world's Navies, and the Royal Navy in particular, had been using this system since before WW1, but multi-part ammunition using propellant not encased in a brass casing had not been used in a tank before. Early bag charges were cotton wrapped, like their Naval counterparts, but the difficulties of keeping the bag charge dry led to the development of a water-resistant cellulose outer casing, which was consumed in firing, leaving no residue.

Besides the improved heavy ammunition handling, the other benefit was in crew protection. Casualty rates in WW2 due to dangerous ammunition stowage were horrific.

The system is inherently slower than single round loading, but rigorous training overcame that, *(see later "Living With Chieftain" chapter!)* and the average engagement time per target on the ranges was twelve to fourteen seconds, that also being a sustainable tempo. At a stroke, the problem of loader fatigue disappeared, as did the need to store or eject empty casings, which would also bring fumes into the turret. Without the heavy casing, the propellant and projectile were both light and easy to handle – charge bags are very light in weight. Stowage was simplified and made safer for combat conditions, as the inert projectiles could be stored in nooks and crannies all round the hull, and crucially, above the turret ring. HESH rounds were stowed below the turret ring, while the bag charges were kept as low in the hull as possible, in GRP charge bins, lined with pressurised antifreeze.

The effectiveness of this system was shown in the Iran-Iraq war. When an Iraqi round did manage to penetrate the heavy armour of an Iranian Chieftain's turret, it did not result in an instant and catastrophic explosion of the ammunition. If the pressurised bins were penetrated, and the resulting

Carry That Weight

With the development of Heavy Tanks during and immediately after WW2, gun calibres increased. So did the weight and size of the ammunition, bringing handling difficulties with it. A partial solution was two-part ammunition.

The Soviet IS-2/3 *Josef Stalin* tank had two-part brass canister and projectile ammunition feeding its A-19/D-25T 122 mm gun. This gun was derived from a Naval design, was readily available in quantity, and it had considerable killing power.

But there were trade-offs. Two severe drawbacks were that even a well trained crew – that is to say, still dependent on a single loader – could only fire two to three rounds a minute, while the ammunition supply was limited to just 27 rounds. This was a major deficiency in a tank which was intended to spearhead attacks.

The post-war American M103 Heavy Tank, equipped with a M58 120 mm gun, also used a two-part separate charge and projectile. As with the IS-2, the charge was contained in a brass cartridge. On this tank, the number of rounds was limited to 34. Achieving an acceptable rate of fire required a second loader on board, adding to space limitations, logistics, costs and so on. With two loaders, the maximum firing rate of the gun was thirteen seconds, but this could not be maintained for anything but very short periods of time.

The British FV 214 Conqueror used the same 120 mm gun, but had only one (severely overworked) loader, and the same limited quantity (35 rounds) of two-part canister/round ammunition – but still had a faster rate of fire than the American M-103 with its two loaders. British Gunnery training proving once again it was the best in the world.

FV 214 Conqueror (Crown Copyright, via Wikimedia Commons)

Josef Stalin IS-3 at Kubinka Museum (Phil Cater)

M103 Heavy Tank at 3rd Cavalry Museum, Fort Hood, Texas. (SkaarupHA, via Wikimedia Commons)

11

Dropping Charges

During secret Troop trials conducted by 1st and 5th RTR over the winter of 1962, a rift rapidly developed between the trials crews and the gunnery design team (who mostly had Royal Artillery backgrounds) about the loading of the main gun. This dispute centred on the electro-mechanical rammer, which the designers had installed to complete the loading of the bag charge. The loader was supposed to load the projectile into the breech, then place the bag charge onto the rammer, allowing it to complete the loading cycle. This was a clumsy, slow and impractical method. The rammer also had a mind of its own, and would start the ramming sequence when it felt like it, trying to feed the loader into the breech, or just not working at all.

Both trials crews independently came up with the same idea (now known as charge ramming) whereby the projectile was loaded into the breech, followed by the bag charge then being pushed up behind it by hand. This was much simpler and faster than using the unreliable mechanical rammer.

The argument was long and bitter, with the design team insistent that manual charge ramming was dangerous, and that pressing on the bag charge igniter pad would have terrible consequences, such as plague, pestilence and fire, or at least exploding bag charges.

To break the deadlock between the two sides, the trials crews invited the entire design team to a demonstration of both methods of loading at the Hohne range complex. On arrival at the designated site early in the morning, the designers were directed to look up at the top of the approximately thirty metre-high range viewing tower, which had just appeared out of the clearing mist. At the top was a trial crew member, holding a bag charge, igniter pad facing down, over the side of the tower.

After a short pause for effect, the attention of those looking up suddenly focused, as they realised the bag charge was about to be dropped from the side of the tower. The design team scattered in all directions seeking cover, while the RTR trial crew remained motionless. The bag charge hit the ground on its igniter pad, but did not explode.

After such a convincing demonstration, the charge ramming system was adopted and the electro-mechanical rammer removed. Manual loading is still employed today on Challenger 2.

Bergen-Hohne Range 7B with range tower in foreground. (Hajotthu via Wikimedia Commons)

Range panorama of Bergen-Hohne tank firing range SB 1A with tank targets and the training village Heidedorf. (Hajotthu, via Wikimedia Commons)

Mk 1 front view.
(Charlie Pritchett)

antifreeze spray did not actually stop the charges igniting, it hissed loudly, venting white smoke, but containing the fire for up to fifteen minutes, allowing surviving crew time to evacuate, saving many lives.

Crew protection was central to the tank's design, and this overriding requirement prompted the decision that the turret control systems would be electro-mechanical, as opposed to hydraulic. Hydraulic systems are highly pressurised, and when hit, spray a fine mist of flammable oil all round the turret interior, which then ignites, and either triggers an ammunition explosion destroying the tank, or horrifically burning the crew. An electro-mechanical system does not have this weakness, but is more complicated to maintain and intrinsically less stable than hydraulics, but this was a trade-off the designers were willing to accept.

Vickers-Armstrongs continued to make progress on the turret, which also had many unique design features. Like the hull front, the front third of the turret was a single casting, incorporating a sophisticated low-slung (for a Western tank) ballistic shape, proof against any existing Soviet anti-tank round. This casting took over twelve months to cool before it could be welded to the rest of the turret.

It had always been intended that the new tank would have the best fire control equipment available, to take advantage of the long range and stopping power of the new L11 120 mm gun. This included a laser rangefinder. However, development of such a device proved more difficult than anticipated. This was one of the few turret systems running behind schedule, so, as an interim measure, it was decided to fit a .50 calibre ranging gun. The Browning M2 was available off the shelf, but in another incomprehensible decision, the new American M85 was specified – this was an untried design, which proved more dangerous to its users than any enemy, with a tendency to suffer breech explosions. It was quickly dropped, and the excellent M2 Browning used instead.

Mk 1 side view.
(Charlie Pritchett)

General Purpose Machine Gun

The GPMG or "Gimpee" as it's fondly nicknamed, is a superb weapon – reliable and dependable, with a high rate of fire, and very accurate. Barrels can be changed in seconds on the standard Infantry GPMG, and it is easy to maintain. The Chieftain used two distinct types. The L8A2 was the co-axial machine gun, fired electronically, not having a standard trigger mechanism fitted. It also had a much thicker barrel, which lasted much longer than a normal Infantry version would. The reason for this was that changing the barrel of a GPMG installed in its co-axial mount was very difficult, nigh impossible. A flash suppressor was also permanently fitted, and this is what can be seen protruding outside of the turret to the side of the main gun.

The commander's GPMG was the L37A2, which is almost identical to the standard Infantry L7A2, other than the inclusion of a feed pawl depressor to aid feeding a new belt in without opening the top cover. The L37A2 had a standard trigger mechanism, as it was designed to be removed and used in a ground role if the tank had to be abandoned. It also had a carry handle attached and a bipod and detachable butt provided, to convert it into an Infantry weapon. In an operational situation, the bipod and butt would be stuck to the top of the commander's sight housing, using "black nasty" – the British Army version of duct tape. For peacetime exercises, they were wrapped up in black plastic bags to keep them clean (as were all the crew's personal weapons, except one used for guard duty, shared by all crew members) and stored safely in the turret.

Complaints by RAC Regiments that the constant changing of the single 200 round ammunition boxes added extra unnecessary work for the already busy loader prompted the design of the "Banana Bin", which allowed multiple boxes of ammunition to be linked together around the cupola for the commander's machine gun. Unfortunately, they were not effective, as the design allowed the ammunition to kink and jam, so most Chieftains retained the single box feed until they went out of service. The Berlin Brigade Chieftains were all fitted with "Banana Bin" commander's MG feed trays from the mid-1980s.

A standard L7 GPMG almost identical to the L8 Commander's GPMG. (RK Collection)

An L8 with permanently attached flash suppressor, and the Stirling SMG or 'Star Wars' gun – for many years the personal weapon of tank crews. (RK Collection)

Close up of an L8 or L37 A1, showing the feed pawl which allowed reloading without lifting the cover. (RK Collection)

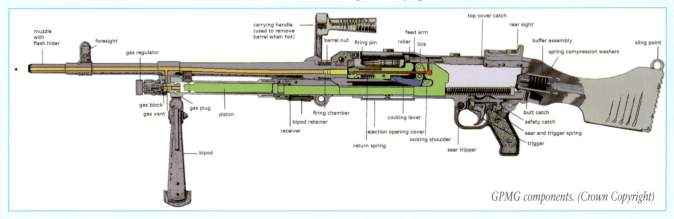

GPMG components. (Crown Copyright)

The prototypes and Mk 1 Chieftain used the Browning .30 calibre machine gun as the Co-axial and commander's machine guns, but these venerable weapons proved disappointing in trials on the new tank, while also adding another non-standard ammunition type to the logistics train. In another effort to spread standardisation among NATO Armies, the Belgian FN General Purpose Machine Gun (GPMG) 7.62 mm (NATO's then standard ammunition size) was adopted, as it was also being introduced into the Infantry as their standard light and heavy support machine gun. Fortunately, this time, it proved to be an excellent choice.

Early progress on the turret design began to be delayed by constant revisions of requirements from the Ministry of Supply/War Office. For example, adding the need for a night fighting capability, using an Infrared searchlight, which was bolted on, like the afterthought it was, onto the left side of the turret. Initially, on the prototypes and Mk 1, it was mounted in a heavy armoured barbette, but from the Mk 2, this was changed to an unarmoured one, to save weight – which would have made it one of the first things rendered unserviceable in any real battle.

More time was wasted redesigning the turret to make it interchangeable with the American 90 mm-gunned T-95 turret. The flawed logic in changing it for one of inferior design – and with a smaller gun as well – seemed to have escaped the designers, who were very enamoured with this idea, but fortunately, the Americans cancelled the T-95, and with it, the turret exchange project. A rudimentary NBC over-pressure system was bolted to the rear, which helped to balance the weight of the turret with its long gun. Some cynical tank crews suggested it was additional spaced armour, as it was not much use in its actual job, and would be replaced with an improved version on the late Mk 3.

The gun control equipment also included a contra-rotating cupola, with an independent sight, and, from the Mk 2 onward, the ability for the commander to override the gunner and lay and fire the main gun, or co-axial machine gun fixed above it, if required. An analogue ballistic computer was also fitted later in the vehicle's service life, as were improved sights – all designed to make full use of the astounding range and accuracy of the main gun.

The Ministry of Supply, by now renamed the War Office, had authorised two batches of prototype vehicles to be built – P1 to P6 starting in 1960, and six more, W1 to W6, delivered between March 1961 and February 1962. All these vehicles were almost constantly being reworked and updated, but it was considered that by late 1962, the FV 4201, now christened Chieftain, was ready for user trials.

In late December 1962, under conditions of great secrecy, two vehicles (W1 and W3) were delivered – one each to The 1st and 5th Royal Tank Regiments, for independent three month user trials in West Germany. The trials crews were initially impressed with the new tanks, but soon began to find faults. Long lists of deficiencies were presented, in two independently written assessments. These were much

When Smoke Gets In Your Eyes

Smoke Dischargers, or to give them their long-winded official title – *Multi Barrelled Smoke Grenade Dischargers* (MBSGD) were common to most British AFVs from the 1950s, and Chieftain was no exception. Initially, a modified set of Centurion smoke dischargers was used, but from the Mk 1, a new cast design, designated Mk 7 MBSGD, was fitted. This had six barrels, able to fire various types of grenade. Trials of the new system highlighted a flaw in the coverage of the smoke, and a revised type known as the Mk 9 came into service with the Chieftain Mk 2 from 1965. One discharger was mounted on each side of the turret face. They were fired either in unison or individually by the gunner pressing the firing buttons to his right hand side. The favoured grenade was the L8, which burst in mid-

Smoke discharger with dummy grenades in place. (RK)

air and contained white phosphorus, creating an instant smokescreen, 102.5° wide, allowing the tank to (hopefully) reverse out of trouble.

By the end of Chieftain's career, the smoke dischargers had fallen out of favour, as the Thermal Observation and Gunnery System (TOGS) could see right through a smokescreen – as the Iraqis found to their cost when faced with TOGS equipped Challengers in the First Gulf War. It was assumed – apparently incorrectly – that Russian tanks would have thermal imaging systems with similar capabilities.

On the Mks 1-5, the smoke dischargers were fixed in place, but with the introduction of Stillbrew armour cladding on the Mk 10 they had to be relocated, and a new swinging mount developed, to allow clearance for the engine decks to be opened (the turret had to be traversed to the side to allow access to the engine decks). When not in use, a canvas cover was placed over them to keep the tubes clean.

Pencil sketch of a Mk 1 Chieftain, highlighting the full width rear bins. Early split hatch No. 11 cupola, jerry can rack instead of stowage bin, no stowage basket. (Crown Copyright)

to the dismay of the Cavalry Brigadier in charge of the project, who tried to suppress the reports, demanding the trials crews rewrite them in a more favourable light, in order that the Chieftain could go into immediate production. The Royal Tank Regiment refused to be intimidated, and the reports were submitted in their original form, which, while delaying the in-service date of the Chieftain, meant it was a much better tank when it did arrive. The War Office accepted the findings, ordering many of the recommendations in the reports to be implemented. Although it did allow production to begin before all the improvements were embodied, to get the Chieftain into service, as it was years late by this point. The Chieftain was officially accepted into service on 1st May 1963.

Mk 1 armoured searchlight – note strange opening design. (R. Griffin)

Prototype P6 at Bovington Reserve Collection (Phil Cater)

Soldier Magazine trumpeting the Army's new Tank, the photo is of a prototype Chieftain.

The full range of British ammunition. The blue ones are training rounds. (Crown Copyright)

However, it seems the Brigadier got his revenge, as the 1st and 5th RTR were originally intended to be the first Regiments issued with the Chieftain, but instead, a Cavalry Regiment – the 11th Hussars – were nominated to be the first to be equipped. The Commanding Officer of this unit then wrote a sycophantic report on how wonderful, reliable and quiet the new tank was – completely at odds with the reality of the situation. But at least the 'Men In Black' (RTR) had told it like it was.

The original armoured searchlight housing. Note centre opening hinge. (RK)

Who Designed Chieftain?

An information plaque at the Tank Museum, Bovington, credits the design of the Chieftain to Mr Leslie Monger MBE. Surely if he had not passed onto the Green Fields, then he would be insisting on having the caption changed and his name removed, as Chieftain was a joint effort utilising the talents of many different designers and companies. Nevertheless, it is certainly true that Leslie Monger MBE is one of the great unsung heroes of British armoured vehicle development, overseeing the progress of the Centurion, Chieftain, FV 432 APC family and CVR(T), to name just a few of the vehicles he had a hand in developing.

Very little information is known about him. Possibly some details are still secret, but his name and reputation was known to those "in the know" about British AFV development from the 1940s to the late 1970s. What little is publicly known comes from the hard to find book *Modern Combat Vehicles 1 – Chieftain*, by Col. George Forty, and is abridged below.

Leslie or Les Monger began his career working for companies such as Thorneycroft and Leyland Motors; he joined the Department of Tank Design in 1941 and spent the next three years trying to improve the woeful quality of the current crop of British tanks. In late 1943, he was transferred to the design team working on Centurion. In 1948, he became the Chief Engineer of the Concept Design Group, which oversaw the development of all British armoured vehicles, and remained in this post for 24 years. During his tenure, he oversaw the golden age of British tank and AFV development. During the period 1972-1976 he was not only in charge of the Concepts Design Group, but also the Technical Control Committee for the Joint West German/British Future Main Battle Tank programme. He was awarded the MBE in 1975, and soon after this, retired after 35 years.

Leslie Monger (British)

Designed
Chieftain, the British main battle tank of the Cold War period, 1950s-1980s.

Les Monger's anonymous plaque at Bovington.

Such an outstanding contribution to British tank and AFV development should more appropriately have been acknowledged with a Knighthood, rather than an MBE.

Chapter Two

Chieftain Production

Only forty Chieftain Mk 1s were built, twenty-six by Royal Ordnance Factory Leeds, and fourteen by Vickers-Armstrongs in Newcastle. These vehicles were never intended to go into service, and were very different from the Mk 2. The Mk 1 had a unique shape, and was shorter than the production tanks. Other differences included the engine decks and commander's cupola, among hundreds of other variations, the most obvious being the low ground clearance of only seventeen inches (43 cm). User trials had highlighted the fact the Chieftain would bottom out and stick in the mud due to this low clearance, and the flat-hulled underside. The Mk 1 was only used for troop trials and training, never being issued to Royal Armoured Corps (RAC) Regiments.

The first "real" Chieftain was the Mk 2, and it was a very different beast to the Mk 1. The Mk 2 was also in a constant state of development, as feedback was received from continuing trials at various establishments, and from service in RAC Regiments. The ride height had been cleverly increased by swapping the road wheels with larger Centurion wheels (which also saved money as existing stocks could be used) and by adjusting the height of the drive sprocket and idler wheel, which gained an extra five inches of clearance, for only a one inch (2.5 cm) increase in overall height. The lower hull was also given a slight 'V' shape (or 'boat bottom') to help prevent it sticking to mud. As related in later chapters on BATUS, and the Iranian Operation *Nasr*, the risk – and severe consequences – of getting bogged down still remained.

All that remains. The factory gate, Austhorpe Road. (Openplaques.org)

The engine silencers were relocated to an armoured box on the rear of the tank outside the engine compartment, to help keep the gearbox cool. The engine decks were extensively reworked, also for improved cooling, and to clear the increased height of the enlarged L60 engine pack. This was the most significant improvement over the Mk 1, now with an engine capable of producing 650 hp in the later Mk 2s.

Building a Chieftain hull inside ROF Leeds. (RK Collection)

The first Mk 2 was delivered on 18th April 1966, but the 11th Hussars did not receive their first Chieftain until November, as the tanks required extensive reworking to bring them up to the required standard. The Mk 2 was also trial-fitted with a deep wading kit, as the design brief maximum weight of 45 tons was never close to being achieved. The all-up weight of a Mk 2 was almost 53 tons – too much for most bridges of the time. Later improvements in German bridge carrying capacity meant the wading kit was only ever fitted to one Mk 2 in trials, although vestiges of the kit somehow survived throughout the rest of the Chieftain's production run. These were the seemingly pointless U-shaped rail on the glacis, and two hooks on the right hand side hull, to secure the boarding ladder. The trials highlighted the severe psychological pressure placed on the driver, ploughing his way blind through deep muddy water, with no rapid means of escape, while also being dependent on the unreliable engine.

The Mk 2 was continuously developed and refined during its service life – there were six official sub-Marks – and to further confuse matters, every Chieftain was reworked to the latest standard as they returned to Base Workshops or the factory for overhaul. This constant upgrading process is what makes identifying the actual Mark of any given Chieftain almost impossible – unless you have its registration number, and the year the photo was taken – and even then, you may still be wrong!

The Mk 3 introduced another slew of improvements, mainly connected with the running gear and engine ancillaries, as the basic Mk 3 form.

Above, Left: Hull Line (Tank Museum, Bovington)

Above: Turret Line (Tank Museum, Bovington)

More modifications soon followed, resulting in eighteen sub-marks between May 1971 and February 1972, when production of the Mk 3 ceased.

The most important changes were a further improved L60 pack, now able to produce 720 bhp – while it lasted, as every increase in power seemed to be accompanied by a corresponding decrease in reliability. Other modifications included an uprated NBC pack and improved gunner's sight.

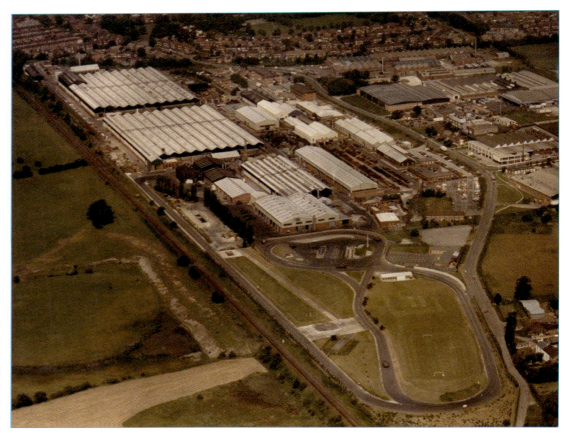

Royal Ordnance Factory Leeds, where all Chieftain Gun tanks were built. Note several tanks on the test circuit. Now a housing estate, and single large empty warehouse. (RK Collection)

Only two Mk 4s were built. This type was intended as the Israeli Chieftain, and was modified to suit their particular needs. It is fully described in the later 'Foreign Sales' chapter. Both tanks were later used by the British Army.

The Mk 5 was the culmination of all that had gone before, and the point at which the design, previously the Mk 3/3, was supposedly frozen, renamed Mk 5, and put into large scale production. It is ironic that the vast majority of Mk 5s went to Iran and Kuwait, with the British Army receiving relatively few, upgrading its own fleet to Mk 5 standard over time. Although there are several subsequent Marks and sub-Marks, they are all reworkings of older vehicles. The last new-build Chieftain was a Mk 5, although even that has six sub-Marks.

The Mk 5/1 saw the installation of the Tank Laser Sight, and removal of the .50 ranging gun to the right of the main gun barrel (as viewed from the front). Many ex-Chieftain crewmen consider this a mistake, as the higher calibre ranging gun was perfect for engaging soft targets such as APCs. The co-axial 7.62 mm machine gun and commander's 7.62 mm GPMG are incapable of destroying these, which meant a main gun round would have to be wasted instead. It is telling that the export versions of the Mk 5 had both TLS and ranging gun.

There was also a Mk 5/3P, which was a deceptive designation to hide the changes made to the Chieftain as the first part of the FV 4030 upgrade programme for Iran. Differing sources suggest either 187 or 191 of these were built.

Almost a thousand Chieftains were manufactured for the British Army, and a similar number for export. While the exact number is unknown, it is generally accepted that approximately 2,265 Chieftains were built in total, between 1965 and 1985.

The Mk 5 was the last "new" build Chieftain. All gun tanks which left the ROF Leeds from 1972 were to this build standard. The later Mk 6, 7, 8, 9, 10 and 11 are re-workings of the original Mk 2 – Mk 5 fleet to various standards and were undertaken at the REME Base workshops in BAOR (West Germany) and in the UK.

The Royal Ordnance Factory, Barnbow, Leeds, built all Chieftain Gun Tanks while the privately owned Vickers-Armstrong (latterly Vickers BAE Systems) in Newcastle, with its higher unit costs, built the special purpose vehicles which had usually been designed and tested at Barnbow. Sadly both factories no longer exist and with their passing the United Kingdom does not have the technological ability or facilities to build and develop its own indigenous tanks and armoured fighting vehicles. A situation that is a national disgrace for the nation that invented the tank.

Chapter Three
Chieftain Development in the British Army

The first Chieftains went into Regimental service in November 1966 with the 11th Hussars, shortly followed by the 17/21st Lancers, after which they began to replace the Centurion at an increasing rate in the British Army of the Rhine's (BAOR) Armoured Regiments. When it entered service, Chieftain became the most powerful tank in NATO, and remained so for over twenty years, until the Leopard 2 entered service with a 120 mm smoothbore main gun. Even then, it remained arguably superior to the early versions of the Leopard 2, introduced into service in 1979, indicating how far ahead of its time Chieftain actually was.

If the Chieftain's armour and 120 mm gun impressed its allies, it shocked the Soviets, who scrambled to find out all they could about the capabilities of the tank. Regiments equipped with the Chieftain in the late 1960s and early 1970s played a cat and mouse game with Russian SOXMIS (permitted free ranging military observer) teams and agents. Stories are told about the wife of a Cavalry Regiment Commanding Officer chasing one SOXMIS team away from a tank park – on horseback! The Soviets soon understood that, at a stroke, their entire tank force had been rendered obsolete, and began a crash programme to develop new missiles, tank main guns and ammunition which could defeat the Chieftain's armour, and match or exceed its range. It is a fact that the Group of Soviet Forces Germany (GSFG) had its best armoured units and equipment, such as the T-64 and later T-80, positioned in northern Germany, facing the British and their Chieftains, rather than further south, facing West German Leopard 1s or American M60s.

The Mk 2, although by far the most numerous model used by the British Army, was always considered an interim model. It was used as an in-service test bed, incorporating most of the modifications

A heavily modified (upgraded) Mk 2 which still retains its single headlights and full width splash guard. Duxford IWM Land Warfare Hall. (RK)

Mk 5 with the hated Dozer blade fitted. (RK Collection)

arising from regular user trials. These included the completely redesigned commander's cupola (No. 15 Mk 1) with a single rearward opening hatch, instead of the split hatches of the Mk 1. It was also the only version of the Chieftain that was designed to use deep wading equipment, which was (mostly) dispensed with from the Mk 3 onwards, being considered unnecessary, if not downright dangerous, as previously noted. There are several sub-Marks of the Mk 2, in common with all Chieftain variants, but many of these were created retrospectively, as the early Marks received upgrades, to bring them to the definitive Mk 5/4 standard.

The Mk 3 introduced oil-filled axle arms, and a raft of other automotive improvements to cope with the increased weight of the tank over its original design brief. (Now standing at 54 tons in service, as opposed to the 45 tons originally intended.)

The main identification points between a Mk 2 and Mk 3 are as follows: there is a hexagonal nut in the end of the road wheel and idler wheel hubs of the Mk 3 onwards, while the Mk 2 hub came to a point, but just to further confuse things, the Mk 2 had the uprated axle arms retrofitted when over-hauled. Another change on the later Mk 3s was the headlights, which swapped the single white lights of the Mk 1/Mk 2 for a dual white light/infra-red setup.

The IR night-fighting equipment was not popular with crews, as it was an active system, which made them a glowing target for anyone with an IR detector. The searchlight was a standard white light

D Sqn 1 RTR Mk 11 at full speed down the pylon line on the Soltau training area. Note the non-tactical NAAFI wash bowl. (RK)

unit, with a simple plastic red cover which filtered out all but the IR wavelengths. The filter could be folded away into the cover, allowing the full power of the white light to be used. The driver and commander both had sights which were changed for IR versions when night fighting. A tactic was worked out where one tank per troop would "illuminate" the battlefield, and the others engage any targets thus revealed, which prevented all the tanks being exposed, but one can imagine how the "illuminating" crew felt about that! Often on exercise, crews would simply use the white light rather than change their sights. This was called "Go White Go Hard", reflecting the speed with which things happened – the illuminating crew would not keep their searchlight on for long...

The commander controlled the searchlight, which could pivot upwards, and the hinged filter and cover, via a small box with simple toggle switches next to his seat. In the Mk 2, the searchlight had also been used just to provide the drivers with IR illumination via their sights when driving at night. Following advice from the Israelis, two small IR headlights were fitted, as these were more difficult for an enemy to see.

The commander also had a small hand operated white light/IR searchlight fitted to the No. 15 cupola. Why this was installed, and what its original use was intended to be, is unclear. It was not linked in elevation with the commander's GPMG. The author only ever saw it being flashed to represent firing the main gun on exercise. All in all, a pretty useless piece of kit.

The Mk 3 also had an improved engine of 650, later 720, bhp compared to the barely adequate 585 bhp of the Mk 2, and several other improvements, mostly related to the engine cooling fans. The turret had a new version of the No. 15 commander's cupola, with increased elevation for his machine gun, to provide some limited anti-aircraft capability. Although many commanders considered the idea of engaging something like a Hind D attack helicopter which had you in its sights with anything less than the main gun as futile, but comforting!

The Mk 3/S (for Sandman) was the embodiment of the information and recommendations from the Israeli trials of the Chieftain, and is externally indistinguishable from the Mk 3/3. They were intended to fulfil an order placed by Libya, the details of which are outlined later in this book. The forty tanks built were diverted to British Army stocks.

The Mk 3/3 was the final version of the Mk 3 line, with a heavily redesigned engine, now capable of 720 bhp (750 bhp in export versions), and was the last of what might be called the development Chieftains. In February 1972, the design was supposedly frozen to allow mass production to begin. By the end of Mk 3 production for the British Army in October 1971, (+ 44 Mk 3/3P (for Persia) built for Iran between October 1971 and February 1972) the Chieftain had been in operational service for four years.

As outlined in the preceding Chapter, the two Mk 4s were taken into service by the British Army, following cancellation of the deal with Israel. They were sent to the proving grounds in Yuma, Arizona, where they performed very well in the hot and high desert conditions. One was later destroyed in mine resistance trials. The fate of the other is uncertain, although for many years it worked at the Kirkcudbright ranges with standard tracks fitted, and a Coles crane in place of the turret. The latest reliable information is that it was written off in an accident when it rolled into a ditch, and was subsequently used as a hard target on the range.

Initially, the Mk 5 was identical to the Mk 3/3, with the same 720 bhp engine, an improved exhaust system, revised air filters, battery heating and lagging, redesigned and increased ammunition storage, and improved gunner's and commander's sights. It also had an improved NBC pack (No. 6 Mk 1) which actually kept out the nasties, to list but a few of the modifications incorporated into the "final" design. The majority of new-build Mk 5 production was diverted to foreign sales and the British Army gradually reworked its mixed fleet up to Mk 5/4 standard during the regular base workshop overhauls.

Nevertheless, the Mk 5 did not escape the constant tinkering which characterised the whole Chieftain programme.

The Mk 5/1 saw the introduction of the new Clansman radio system, replacing Larkspur. Tanks fitted with Clansman originally had a C suffix after their designation, dropped once the entire fleet was converted. These can be identified by the rectangular box welded to the left side of the turret, in front of the commander's bin, with the antenna base mounted on top of it – the forward Larkspur antenna base is blanked off.

The Mk 5/1 also finally saw the introduction of the long awaited Tank Laser Sight (TLS) and with it, the ability to fully exploit the L11A5 120 mm main gun's exceptional range and accuracy. The L11 holds the record for the longest ever recorded tank kill, at 5.3 km (3.3 miles). Admittedly this was with an L11 fitted to a Challenger 1 in the Gulf War, but the gun and much of the fire control equipment was identical to the Chieftain's.

The ranging machine gun (RMG) was retained in the Mk 5/1, but deleted on the Mk 5/2, with its improved TLS. The Mk 5/2 also introduced the Muzzle Reference System, which measured barrel distortion. This can be identified by the shroud, which looks like a rifle foresight on the end of the barrel, and a rectangular box to the right of the gunner's main sight. When repeatedly fired, the gun could get hot and "bend", due to differential cooling (wind blowing on one side of the gun, for example). This changed the gun-to-sight relationship, causing a round to miss – a couple of millimetres of barrel distortion would translate to a two or three metre difference at the target point. To correct this, a mirror was attached to the end of the barrel, covered under the previously mentioned shroud. With the camo netting removed from the barrel, a light projector fired a beam of red light at the mirror, which reflected back to the projector, revealing any offset. This would then be automatically compensated for by the ballistic computer (it moved the target eclipse in the sight, in simple terms) so the gun remained accurate.

The Mk 5/3 had the Improved Fire Control System (IFCS), which tied the MRS, TLS and the new sights fitted, to exploit the L11 gun's abilities with an analogue ballistic computer and other fire control tweaks. These fire control improvements really did make Chieftain dominant on the battlefield, far ahead of anything fitted to any other tank of the era, Western or Soviet. If the Chieftain had been called upon to fight an advancing Soviet onslaught, it would surely have taken a heavy, and quite possibly decisive, toll on the Soviet armoured spearheads. It might even have managed the 15:1 kill ratio which crews were soberly informed would be necessary "if the balloon goes up"...

A programme called Totem Pole was introduced in 1971 to unify the fleet to a common Mk 5/4 standard. This was a three-phase upgrade, imaginatively sub-titled X, Y and Z. X was updating of the fire

Even when the engine wasn't smoking, the Chieftain could make a huge dust cloud.
(J. McConnell)

control system, while Y and Z dealt with the automotive side. The intent was for Base Workshops to do the work, but this proved too much for them to handle alongside their normal workload, so special field lines were set up at Main Base and UK Command Workshops. Inevitably, some Chieftains in remote locations were missed, and these are now very rare and valuable escapees, but the great majority were upgraded, and became indistinguishable from the Mk 5.

The last variant of the Mk 5, the Mk 5/4, introduced a new type of ammunition, Armour Piercing Fin Stabilised Discarding Sabot (APFSDS), also known as Freddy Fin, or just 'Fin'. This made the gun even more lethal, capable of penetrating the armour of any tank at extreme range – perfect for the Chieftain, with its niche as a long-range sniper. The new ammunition required further modifications to the stowage, and new sight graticules. When firing this type of round, the whole 54 tons of tank could be felt to lift off its tracks and recoil backwards as it left the barrel – but it also stripped the rifling at a rapid rate. This was belatedly discovered during the 1991 Gulf War build-up, where free use of full power service ammunition contrasted with the miserly issue of reduced charge training rounds issued in Germany. Many Chieftains donated their barrels to the Challenger 1 fleet, as spares rapidly depleted in-theatre. Additionally, the driver's hatch had to be closed down when firing 'Fin', to prevent severe injury. In this, its final form, the Chieftain Mk 5/4 was the backbone of the Armoured Regiments of BAOR and the defence of Northern Germany for almost twenty years.

The Mk 5/4 was the definitive Mark of Chieftain. The production line at Royal Ordnance Factory Leeds began turning out large numbers for both the British Army, and for export – the first of which rolled out in March 1972, and the last in late 1985.

The Mark 6, 7 and 8 were renamings of Marks 2, 3, 3S and 3/3, rebuilt to full Mk 5/4 specification on completion of the Totem Pole programme.

The Mk 9 was a blanket renaming of the entire Chieftain fleet after it had been brought up to Mk 5/4 standard, and the full APFSDS ammunition fit-out completed.

The Mk 10 saw the first major external visual changes to Chieftain in twenty years, with the addition of new armour. Beginning in August 1984, the Stillbrew up-armouring package developed by Colonel Still and Mr John Brewer of the Fighting Vehicle Engineering Establishment (FVEE) was introduced. It had been accepted by MOD that due to the repeated failures of various replacement initiatives (FMBT, MBT 80, ad nauseam...) that the Chieftain was becoming obsolescent, but would have to soldier on for some years yet. While its gun was still unsurpassed with the new munitions and TOGS, its armour had become vulnerable to the new Soviet anti-tank rounds and missiles – which had, after all, been developed especially to counter the Chieftain.

The FVEE had been tasked with developing an up-armouring package, but it was not considered a priority project – at least not until the outbreak of the Iran-Iraq war, where the sight of Chieftains with their frontal armour penetrated helped to concentrate minds at the MOD. As usual, there was no money available from HM Treasury, so with typical British ingenuity, using what were basically old car tyres,

scrap metal and a skim of concrete over the top, Stillbrew was born. This improvised up-armouring package partially protected the turret ring, by addition of armour blocks either side of the Driver. The turret frontal arc was protected with a set of steel boxes, filled with layers of rubber sheets and armour plate fitted to the turret front, increasing the width of the turret. A skim of concrete was used to blend the boxes to look like a single piece, with the boxes sculpted and shaped to give access to the engine decks and gunner's emergency sight aperture. Stillbrew added one and a half tons to the all-up weight, but had no measurable effect on automotive performance.

Stillbrew exposed – steel and rubber, not composite armour. (Rob Griffin)

Despite its somewhat Heath Robinson character, it proved to be extremely effective in trials conducted in the 1990s, using a T-80 and the Russian versions of APFSDS and HESH ammunition, apparently purchased from the Ukraine – according to the official story. (The real story of how the British Army acquired the T-80s used in this trial is one worthy of a John le Carre book!) Stillbrew withstood direct hits at anything up to point-blank range (in tank terms). Each section of the armour could be expected to take at least two, and usually three, hits before failing. It was fitted by Base Workshops as Chieftains came in for their regular overhauls, until the entire active service fleet had been upgraded. The rumour that Stillbrew was an early form of Chobham composite armour was disinformation from the British Government, which has since been accepted as fact.

Alongside the Stillbrew package, new side skirts, incorporating Dorchester 1 (Chobham) armour were also designed. An order was placed for several hundred sets, although later reduced, then (possibly) cancelled.

The new Thermal Observation and Gunnery System (TOGS) was installed in a two-piece armoured barbette in place of the obsolete searchlight. This upgrade, which first began in 1983 on Challenger, then embodied on Chieftain some two years later, gave it a new lease of life, transforming it into a night fighting, all-weather, battle winning weapon. The intention was to refit the entire Chieftain fleet to Mk 11 standard, but the end of the Cold War and collapse of the Soviet Union meant only 311 to 324 (sources vary on this) were upgraded.

The TOGS system was also passive, so not betraying any sign of its operation – extremely useful, given the defensive battles and long range sniping which Chieftain was designed for. TOGS major advantage over image intensifying (II) systems was that it is a thermal imager, which shows the differences in heat between objects, rather than magnifying available light. This allows TOGS to "see" even when there is no light to magnify and through smoke screens or dense natural smoke, which would blind II systems. TOGS was able to give accurate range to target info, far beyond that of even the much vaunted laser rangefinder, which (as discovered in the First Gulf War) could be blocked by

smoke. TOGS was fully integrated with the IFCS, but did require the removal of the commander's contra-rotating cupola equipment, and the loss of some ammunition stowage in the increasingly cramped confines of the turret.

The impact TOGS had on the Chieftain and her successors simply cannot be understated. The system is a battle if not war winner, and the best Thermal Imaging gunnery system in the world. It is still in use, in improved form, on Challenger 2. If some within MOD had had their way, it would never have seen the light of day, but thankfully, the optic specialists Barr and Stroud had the courage to develop it privately, with the encouragement of others in MOD, who insisted on pushing it forward.

Chieftain crews trained on TOGS consistently outshot the new Challenger 1 tanks also fitted with it on the annual gunnery ranges, and in the author's opinion, if the TOGS-equipped Chieftain had been chosen to represent the British Army at the 1987 Canadian Army Trophy, this competition would not have been the debacle it turned out to be.

The Mk 11 was the final, and in many ways, ultimate Chieftain, defined by the the Stillbrew and TOGS combination, which gave the Chieftain an extremely aggressive stance, and it is by far the best looking Chieftain. It just "looks right".

Mk 11 'Boudicca' demonstrated at Bovington. (Peter Trimming, via Wikimedia Commons)

Laser Tag for Big Boys!

Providing realistic training for the Army in peacetime has always been a challenge. The opening of BATUS in Canada in the 1970s alleviated most of the problems, as live ammunition could be used, and in later years, a permanent Opposition Force (OPFOR) was stationed there.

However, the same freedom to use live ammunition was not available in BAOR, and several systems were developed to improve the realism of exercises. These were called Tactical Engagement Simulation Systems. Chieftain used three types during its service. SIMFIRE (Fire Simulator) and SIMFICS (Fire Simulator IFCS) were broadly the same system. SIMFICS incorporated minor improvements to accommodate the IFCS upgrade. Both systems used a laser projector mounted above the main gun to fire laser pulses at "enemy" targets and a bank of pyrotechnic tubes, which fired in unison with the laser, attempting, but miserably failing, to replicate the noise of the main gun firing.

If a hit was made on another SIMFIRE/ SIMFICS equipped vehicle, the receivers mounted at various points on the tank would register it. If the control unit judged it a kill, it would trigger a smoke generator, which would billow orange smoke for all to see. This all sounds wonderful in theory, but in practice, the system was unreliable, temperamental, bulky and cables were strewn everywhere. They were not popular with crews, and in typical Squaddie fashion, ways were soon found to bypass the system to become invulnerable to enemy fire.

By the late 1980s, the systems had almost fallen out of use, but made a comeback with the new DFWES (Direct Fire Weapons Effect Simulator) which was installed on some 1 RTR Chieftains, at the very end of their service in 1995. (1 RTR being the last Regiment in the British Army converted to Challenger 1 – twelve years after it entered service – is possibly due to certain now Senior Officers having long memories, continuing to punish the Men In Black for telling the truth about Chieftain during its troop trials!)

Exactly how DFWES operates remains classified, as it is still in use today, but it is a much improved system, disabling all the tank systems, including the engine, when a hit occurs, supposedly preventing any cheating – unless the crews have found ways around even this system!

Mk 3-2 with SIMFIRE fitted. Note how cam net disguses length of barrel. (RK)

Mk 10 fitted with SIMFICS – note the laser projector mounted over the barrel. (RK Collection)

SIMFIRE detail – laser projector and 'flash bangs' mounted above gun – the clear 'light' is actually the laser reciever. (Phil Cater)

Top: Only known photo of both Mk 4s at Yuma, Arizona. (Rob Griffin)

*Above: One of the Mk 1 tanks converted to an AVLB crossing two overlaid bridges.
(RK Collection)*

*Right: REME demonstrate how the twelve ton turret could be swapped in the field.
(Crown Copyright)*

Mk 2/3 serving with 3 RTR.
(RK)

The sad end for many Chieftains – still used as range targets. (RK Collection)

1 Tp C Sqn 1 RTR Mk 11 – very clean. Note fading to thermal blanket on barrel, exposed TISH, and 56 bridge class – when the tank weighed 62 tons all-up. (RK Collection)

Chapter Four

The Saga of the L60 Engine

As briefly mentioned in the first chapter, the tortured history of the L60 could take up an entire book, but is perhaps best confined here within a single chapter.

The original design specified a conventional V8 Rolls-Royce diesel engine. If only... Early in Chieftain development, it was directed that a multi-fuel engine, as promoted by the NATO Standardisation Committee, would be fitted. While most countries gave lip service to this idea, and developed reliable diesel engines, the British Government embraced it with enthusiasm. They then proceeded to compound their mistake by choosing to develop this new wonder engine from a small vertically opposed pump unit. This was designed by the Rootes Car Group to run at steady revs for long periods, but a tank engine does the opposite – constantly and rapidly changing revs, as it travels across various types of terrain.

The story that the L60 is based on a WWII German Dornier vertically-opposed aircraft powerplant is just that – although it was taken as Gospel truth on tank parks across BAOR. It is certainly a better story than the real one, of government interference and inertia, compounded by design incompetence.

With the decision to pursue the multi-fuel engine option, the Chieftain went from being a world beater to an "also-ran", saddled with one of the most horrifically unreliable engines ever fitted to a tank, which would ruin its reputation, preventing the widespread export success which the Centurion had enjoyed. The new engine also necessitated a complete redesign of the engine compartment, adding weight and height. Almost inevitably, more increases in the engine's size followed, leading to further redesign of the hull, putting the entire project behind schedule, and delaying work on all other aspects of the design. Frustrated with the delays, in August 1958, the Ministry of Supply brought in Vickers-Armstrong as a second main contractor, with responsibility for the turret and armament.

Air intake side of engine.
(RK)

Engine and gearbox exposed – this is a redtop Sundance improved engine, on a privately owned example. (RK)

With responsibility for the turret passed to Vickers-Armstrong, Leyland and Rootes Motors could now concentrate on trying to make the new engine work. They had limited success with a single cylinder test rig, and, by mid-1959, managed to create a full size engine. This leaked like a sieve, shook itself to pieces and stripped its gear train. Incredibly, this was still considered acceptable, and with the engine barely able to make 500 hp, it was fitted to the first prototype vehicle, and gingerly run round the test track. The engine was so severely underpowered, that it proved incapable of driving the tank up the ramps of a tank transporter.

After several years of work, the vibration problems were (mostly) solved, but the L60 leaked fluid throughout its service life. The major problem with the early engines was the lack of power – those fitted into the Mk 2 (the first version to go into service) could only produce 585 bhp, less than two thirds of the initial requirement. The constant problems with the engine had a knock-on effect on vehicle trials. Numerous problems, that could and should have been ironed out during the development stage, instead followed the tank into service. Sadly, many of these issues were never corrected.

These engines should have been pulled out, and all but one scrapped, (with that one retained by Bovington Tank Museum – left there to serve as a salutary warning) and changed for a reliable diesel engine early in the Chieftain's service. This was never done, on immediate cost grounds, and so, over its service life, vastly greater sums were wasted trying to turn a sow's ear into a silk purse. Attempts to rectify the troublesome L60 never stopped. There were more than fourteen distinct versions, which alone indicates just how bad the engine was.

The basic design of a vertically opposed six-cylinder engine was unusual, and why this layout was chosen has never been adequately explained. The perceived wisdom was that it suited a multi-fuel design, but there is no evidence to substantiate this claim. It certainly created difficulties in getting fuel to the cylinders, and keeping the engine oil tight. The engine blocks were painted gloss duck egg blue, in theory, to easily identify the source of an oil leak. In the case of the L60, this only meant the engine became coloured a uniform black, as it leaked from every possible orifice.

The L60 remained incontinent throughout its life, whatever version of engine was installed, partly due to the complexity of the design, and partly due to the engine's tendency to twist and vibrate, which was never adequately addressed. A horizontally opposed (as opposed to vertically opposed) engine would have allowed a much simpler fuel system and oil distribution.

By 1964, the decision had been taken to 'optimise' the engine for diesel due to the unending problems with the multi-fuel requirement. The tipping point was a report by a REME trials team, which stated that it would take at least eight hours to prepare an L60 to accept any other fuel but diesel. Obviously impractical in a war situation.

When one part was fixed or improved, another fault would appear, either in the same system or other parts of the engine. Some had been hidden by the fixed/improved part, while others were caused

L60 front view showing fans and oil tanks above them. (RK)

L60 showing both the notorious fan belts. (RK)

by the fixes! And so, the engineers went round and round in circles, becoming ever more desperate with each new problem – what is referred to within informed engineering circles as cascade failures. The L60 had so many problems, it is easier to simply list the worst aspects, which were:

- Fuel injection pump system (FIPS)
- Pistons
- Cylinder liners
- Manifolds
- Air filtration system
- Exhaust
- Cooling system
- Fans and belts

The system most affected by the myriad changes was the Fuel Injection Pump System (FIPS). Crews, when they could bring themselves to mention the FIPS at all, had their own crude version of what the

L60 side view, including the FIPS. Even this pristine museum exhibit has incontinence stains... (RK)

Leyland L60 on display at Bovington. One radiator raised. (Phil Cater)

initials stood for – something like *Flipping Incontinent Piece of Something*. This highly complex system seemed a classic example of what a mad scientist's imagination could come up with, and your humble author firmly believes its designers really didn't understand how it worked themselves.

The FIPS was always being tinkered with, and "improved". When the decision to abandon the multi-fuel requirement was taken, the increased fuel pressure requirements of diesel put more strain on the system, and these demands only kept on increasing in the quest for ever more power. This caused untold numbers of pump and hose failures, often accompanied by engine fires, as overstressed components failed. The FIPS remained the Achilles Heel of the L60. All the tinkering could not correct the fundamental problem that the system was never designed to cope with the fuel delivery requirements of a 750 bhp 62 ton tank, and it was always under stress.

The pistons were incorrectly shaped for an optimal diesel burn, as was the combustion chamber. The designers thought the maximum temperature reached in the combustion chamber was 300 degrees, when it turned out to be nearer 650 degrees. This led to a complete redesign of the piston crowns with oil cooling incorporated, but again, incomprehensibly, after the multi-fuel requirement had been dropped, the new pistons were not optimised for diesel.

The engine block used cylinder liners to save weight and increase engine life, but this proved to be the engine's biggest, and longest lasting, problem. The basic fault was that whatever material was used to make the liners,

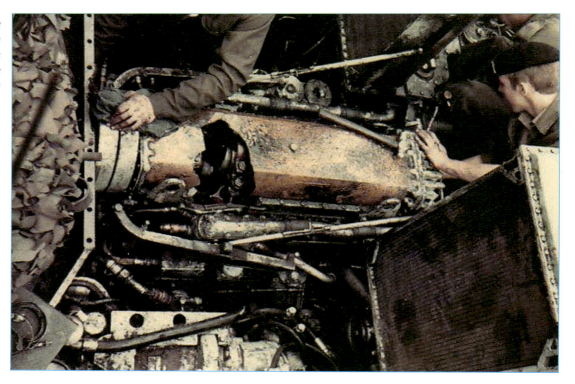

Now, THAT is an engine failure! The piston exited via the crankcase cover. And this was a hand built Sundance engine. (RK Collection)

and however they were secured to the block, they would drop and allow oil and water to mix, with predictable, loud and terminal results.

Even the last so-called "optimal" Mk 14a occasionally suffered from piston liner drop, leading to clouds of white smoke from the already smoky exhausts, soon followed by complete engine failure. Various glues and other fixing methods were tried to stop this happening, none which were completely successful. The material used for the liners was not adequately tested, and was changed dozens of times before a suitable type was found.

When the piston and liner problems had been addressed, the engine was still unable to produce the required levels of power, and this was found in part to be due to the design of the inlet and exhaust manifolds strangling the engine's output. This was only addressed by changing the number of ports.

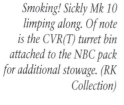

Smoking! Sickly Mk 10 limping along. Of note is the CVR(T) turret bin attached to the NBC pack for additional stowage. (RK Collection)

The engine would now produce around 700 bhp on bench tests, but nothing like that when installed in the tank.

After much head scratching, it was discovered that the airflow to the engine was inadequate – cue hurried modifications to the air cleaner and filtration systems to get sufficient quantities of air into the engine, which still remained inadequate throughout Chieftain's service life. The engine sucked air through the deck louvres, which were redesigned to allow better airflow and shrapnel protection. Mesh screens were added in a failed attempt to stop leaves and debris being sucked into the engine bay and clogging intakes and radiators. Nevertheless, during autumn months, the engine bay could often become clogged with damp soggy leaves, which had to be constantly removed by the crews.

The Israelis suggested using "turret breathing", where air is pulled from inside the turret to feed the engine, as coming from there, it was already "pre-filtered". When closed down during NBC conditions, the engine reverted to pulling air through the louvres. This suggestion was incorporated in the Chieftain from the Mk 3/S onwards.

Air filtration was achieved by a multi-part system, which used cyclonic dust extraction, via a scavenge blower as the first stage, followed by the normal multi layer paper filter, similar but much larger than a vacuum cleaner air filter. (*No – Mr Dyson was never a tank crewman...*) These blowers were changed throughout the Chieftain's life, using either two or three lobe designs to give more power (but less reliability), while further along the pipes, the second stage paper element filter was also improved. Creating a good seal to the engine with this removable barrier filter was very difficult, and if dust got it in, it mixed with the oil, turning into an abrasive paste. This corroded the engine internals, leading to catastrophic but impressive failures, starting with a loud bang, immediately followed by bits of engine cover, pistons and other parts exiting through the engine decks, immobilising a very despondent crew.

The barrier filter was bulky and very heavy, needing two fit men to lift it out of its housing, commonly using their webbing belts as improvised slings. This heavy lifting chore was known as "*Banging out the Biscuit*", and was a regular and vital task to keep the tank running. An experienced driver and his crewmate would do this every time the tank stopped for more than ten minutes. A prime example of the consequences of not doing so, and one they wish forgotten – so I shall repeat it here – is the experience of the Blues and Royals, a Household Cavalry Regiment. Considering themselves elite, they saw fit to decline the well-meant advice of other experienced Chieftain users. They took their brand new steeds to Soltau for the very first time... *Hurrah!! Tally ho!!*... and lost forty out of forty-three within a week to engine failure, rapidly traced to blocked air filters.

Improvements made to the engine air supply highlighted design problems downstream, ending with the exhaust and silencer, which was getting far too hot, and also creating too much back pressure, sapping power from the engine. The excess heat from the exhausts was causing the gearbox, in the same

compartment, to malfunction, although the gearbox itself was laden with its own problems, which are outlined in the next sorry chapter of this book.

The overheating eventually forced another redesign of the rear hull, with the silencers relocated outside in a box on the rear plate, giving Chieftain its distinctive rear end and double exhaust setup. The exhaust pipes initially faced upwards, but given the copious amounts of smoke pouring from them, they were inverted to direct the smoke towards the ground, rather than shooting it high into the sky and giving the tank's location away. An expansion or "smoke box" was fitted above the gearbox, in the space where the silencer had been previously, to help cool the exhaust gases and reduce the back pressure. It still remained hot in the transmission compartment. There was one silver lining in this cloud of acrid smoke. Crews on winter exercises, particularly drivers, could often be seen throwing open the rear transmission decks and sitting inside, pretending to work on something or other, but they were only trying to keep warm!

Early in the engine's development, it was discovered that the cooling requirements had been seriously underestimated (a familiar story in L60 development) and it was hurriedly redesigned, as the first prototypes were meant to be running in a matter of months. This modification was inevitably flawed, but did not come to light until an engine designer happened to overhear an instructor telling new drivers that the left radiator "always ran cold". Further investigation uncovered the fact that Chieftains had, for years, been operating with a huge airlock in their systems, only taking eighteen instead of twenty-five litres of coolant. Fitting bleed valves solved this problem, possibly the simplest fix in the whole chaotic, disorganised and sorry mess that was the L60 programme.

Perhaps the best illustration of the chaos and incompetence that plagued the L60 was the *Saga of the Fan Belts*. From the very beginning, the L60 had a voracious appetite for fan belts, which the designers seemed unable to pinpoint, as when the engine was bench run, failures were rare, but once in the tank, they snapped or shredded constantly. Rather than applying basic engineering fault-finding principles, a series of new fan belts were designed, and yet they still snapped almost as soon as they were fitted. From the 1970s and into the early 1980s, it was rare to see a RTR Chieftain Driver without at least two spare belts round his neck, ready for quick replacement, which many soon had down to a fine art. (It seems the wearing of fan belts by the *Men In Black* was considered poor form by the Cavalry Regiments. The '*Donkey Wallopers*' hung theirs on the turret smoke grenade dischargers instead.)

As the fan belts got stronger and stronger, the stresses were transferred down the line. Eventually, the engine gear cases failed catastrophically before the belts snapped – a much more serious problem. Then, scenes resembling a Monty Python sketch played out across tank parks all over Germany, Canada and the UK. It was directed from Upon High that holes were to be drilled into the new super-strong fan belts – to weaken them.

In the 1980s, someone finally decided to investigate the cause, and not the symptoms. They discovered that the friction clutches designed to slow the fans slowly on shut-down were malfunctioning, due to the still present torsional vibration, slamming the fans to an instant stop, causing the belt to snap.

All but one of the clutches was removed, and that was wired so it could only operate when the auxiliary power unit or "donkey engine" was in use, and the problem disappeared.

The developments, panicked changes, improvisations and redesigning of various parts of the engine described above took place over the entire service life of the Chieftain. These were implemented under a number of programmes given various code names, which reflect some of the air of despondency and frustration which hung over the L60. First, in 1967, came *Scotch Mist,* aiming for a reliable engine, which subtly hints at how likely the engineers thought their chances of success were. This was followed by the infamous *Fleet Foot,* a last ditch attempt in the 1970s to get 750 bhp from the engine, whatever the cost (720 bhp achieved). But after the Mk 7a *Fleet Foot* engines were fitted to the Chieftain, it proved to be so unreliable, the entire fleet was declared VOR (Vehicle Off Road) until a solution was found. A huge embarrassment for the Army and the Government, leaving BAOR without a single tank to defend Northern Germany, a fact of which the Soviets were well aware.

This prompted urgent investigations, undertaken by the Expenditure Committee and Defence and External Affairs Sub-Committee of the House of Commons. A damning report followed – (*THE CHIEFTAIN TANK ENGINE – HMSO London 23 May 1978*). Blame was duly apportioned – "*...in light of the subsequently unfulfilled assurances given by the MOD... [...] The saga of the Chieftain tank does not reflect well on the MOD...*"

This led to the aptly named *Dark Morn* and *High Noon* programmes, addressing the immediate reliability issues, which were resolved to some extent. The *Sundance* programme then followed, which produced an engine that was less fragile and more powerful than any previously achieved.

The resulting Mk 13a and Mk 14a units became known as the "Optimal Engine", which was far from the truth, but certainly represented an improvement over what had gone before, with a marked increase in reliability. Although the 2,500 miles Mean Distance Between Failure target was never met – the average was 2,100 miles – this was still a significant achievement. *Sundance* development engines had a red-painted cylinder head, and crews in tanks fitted with these considered themselves relatively lucky. These units were virtually hand-built and machined to fine tolerances, in contrast to the average engine, which suffered from poor quality control at best, and none at worst, perhaps reflecting the industrial unrest common at that time.

Just about the only automotive component that was of any use at all was the auxiliary generator or "donkey engine", as it was known to the crews. This was a diesel car engine, adapted to provide electrical power to start the main engine, or power the systems when tactically unsound to run the main engine, so saving on fuel and reducing the tank's thermal signature. The large box added above the engine deck of the M1 Abrams in its Tusk II incarnation is just such a device, adopted many years later.

While a flawed design from the outset, not all the problems afflicting the L60 were design issues. Like all engines, it did not like being sat idle for long periods, as they were for most of the time, parked in hangars across West Germany and the UK. Oil seals would dry out, and other parts seize up, with predictable results. In contrast, the Mk 13a and 14a engines in Chieftains issued to BATUS were driven hard over eight to ten months of the year, and proved to be generally reliable. They averaged around 2,700 miles between engine changes, and were also much less smoky than a typical Chieftain issued to an Armoured Regiment in West Germany or the UK.

Chapter Five
The TN12 Gearbox

It is said that lightning never strikes twice. Sadly, this cannot be said of the Chieftain. Already blighted with the L60, the very notion that any other part of the drivetrain could give as much trouble seems almost unbelievable, but the TN12 gearbox tried its very best to match the L60, blow for blow. It was manufactured by Self Changing Gears Ltd, although on the tank park it was always referred to as the David Brown gearbox, usually followed by a wry comment suggesting that he should have stuck to tractors.

The gearbox was designed to be easy to use, and was a semi-automatic type, using a motorcycle style kick change. Simple in theory, but difficult to master in practice – only skilled drivers could ever get a smooth change out of the gearbox by balancing the revs perfectly, and timing their kick to perfection. The unit itself was quite compact, considering the loads it had to transfer. The main brakes were also attached directly to the sides of the gearbox, where the final drives exit. The main (as opposed to steering) brakes were simple but effective disk brakes, but on a much larger scale than those fitted to the average car. These worked well, at least when not covered in oil from the many leaks in the engine bay, and from the gearbox itself. Most crews would have a plumber's gas burner in the toolbox to burn off the oil in the morning when on exercise. This was, of course, strictly forbidden – but done anyway, both out in the field and in the tank parks.

The problems with the gearbox were masked during the trials period, due to the unreliability of the L60. Had the engine been less problematic, there seems a good chance that several of the gearbox problems would have been spotted in time, to allow these to be properly addressed. As it was, cross-country trials took place late in the trials cycle, which was when the myriad gearbox problems came to light. It was massively overcomplicated, and it was a common story that the designer had gone crazy because he didn't understand how it worked either.

The most terrifying way this could manifest itself was with the neutral turn when on level firm ground, such as a tank park. The drivers had to be extremely careful not to touch their steering tillers with the engine running and gearbox in neutral, as the slightest touch would start the tank spinning on the spot. Nothing could stop this rotation, apart from an emergency engine stop. Spinning tanks were generally considered to be a health and safety hazard.

Bovington's instructional cutaway TN-12 gearbox. The silver disk is a main brake, and the circular part at the front the infamous Tyflex coupling – which was a pig to unbolt. (RK)

Pull up a Sandbag...

Another routine day on duty at a tank park, somewhere in West Germany...

No Names, Packdrill or Regiment here – redacted to save people's embarrassment!

XXXX was illegally burning off the oil on the steering pads at the back of the hangar in the troop store, when he carelessly knocked over the five gallon jerrycan he was using. Petrol flooded all round the Troop area, and then burst into flames. Our training kicks in, so we're all panicking, diving out of the way, while breaking Olympic records sprinting away from the fire. The panic spreads, like, er, wildfire, progressing down to 4 Troop, then 3, and so on.

Meanwhile, A and C Sqns are all outside, on the tank park. XXXX picks up the petrol jerrycan, and instead of putting the lid back on, inexplicably flings it outside the hangar. A Catherine wheel of liquid fire careens in an arc, impacts the ground, and a sea of flame then shoots across the compound.

Burning petrol flows into the storm drain in the middle of the park. All the accumulated gunk and oil in the storm drain then ignites, shooting a wall of flame, about six feet high. The storm drain fire starts at B Sqn, and rapidly works its way down the length of the park.

A and C Sqn blokes try to reverse their tanks back into their hangars, to escape the flame danger outside, while B Sqn chaps are frantically trying to get their wagons out of the hangar, to escape from the fire raging inside.

The Adjutant, laconically looking out of his office window, espies a massive black smoke cloud/ wall of flame arising from the storm drain, rapidly heading his way. His officer training kicks in. Doing his best Basil Fawlty meltdown impression, he reacts and instigates the following actions:

- Sets Camp Fire Alarm off. ☑
- German Fire Brigade phoned, and politely requested to attend the incident. ☑
- Guardroom then duly notified, in follow-up telecon, of impending visitors. ☑

The German fire crew were already at the gate, negotiating their entry, having spotted the huge cloud of rising black smoke nearby. The Army Fire Picket, with their hand-pulled fire cart, (wisely) declined to intervene.

Then, a helpful Tannoy Announcement – courtesy of the Guardroom. *"FIRE FIRE FIRE. There is an indicated fire in the B Squadron Area. All personnel are to vacate the building without delay."* ☑

Meanwhile, XXXX is seen running around like a headless chicken, then takes off, running away quickly. It later transpires he's *on fire picket duty*, and had dutifully legged it over to the Guardroom to report.

Can't remember what punishment he got. Of course, XXXX now claims he *"can't remember it at all.."* – but all other ex-5 Troop B Sqn certainly do – *and they all say it was him!*

Needless to say, the German Environmental Inspection Officers (*Die Umweltaufsichtsbehörden*) were not particularly impressed, but I never found out what the result of their investigation was.

Mr. P. Smith (ex-5 Troop B Sqn).

Replacing a gearbox in a German farmyard. Both Chieftains in the photo are under repair and both have interesting and contrasting paint schemes. (RK Collection)

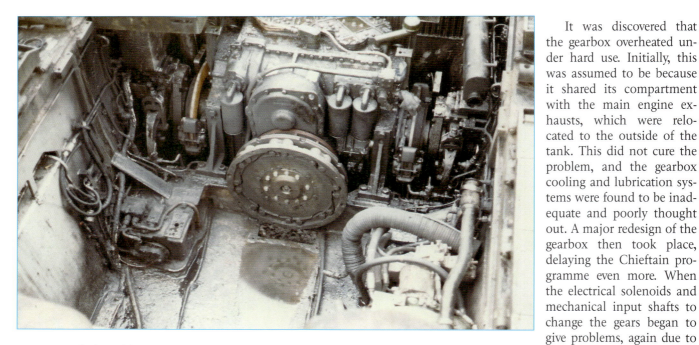

It was discovered that the gearbox overheated under hard use. Initially, this was assumed to be because it shared its compartment with the main engine exhausts, which were relocated to the outside of the tank. This did not cure the problem, and the gearbox cooling and lubrication systems were found to be inadequate and poorly thought out. A major redesign of the gearbox then took place, delaying the Chieftain programme even more. When the electrical solenoids and mechanical input shafts to change the gears began to give problems, again due to

Superb photo of the empty engine compartment showing the TN12. Note the lake of oil deposited in the bottom of the compartment. (H Robinson)

the heat and poor design, there was no time to redesign the system from scratch, and these assemblies gave endless trouble throughout the Chieftain's service.

The underlying problem of all the failures with the gearbox was the fact that the design brief had called for a tank of no more than 45 tons. To save time and money, Self Changing Gears Ltd modified their TN10 gearbox, intended for the cancelled FV 300 *light* tank, with key components strengthened for use in a 45 ton tank. Chieftain, as has been mentioned, was never anywhere close to that weight. If the gearbox had instead been designed from scratch, given the tendency of engineers to over-spec every part, it is likely some built-in redundancy could have allowed the gearbox to cope with some of the extra weight.

Adjoining assemblies, including the final drive shafts, were also prone to failure, for the same reason. As the main brakes depended upon these linkages to stop the tank, such failures were very dangerous to the crew, and anyone unlucky enough to be in the way of an out of control behemoth with no way of stopping.

Chieftain was always a portly girl, and her weight crept up over the years with the various updates and improvements. Stillbrew added a ton and a half, TOGS was heavy too, and the Mk 11 had a fully loaded weight of over 62 tons. Although the small round bridge weight classification on the front would often still say 56, as they had not been repainted since they came into service – Army inertia taking hold! The last Chieftains in service had a bridge weight of 70 painted in the blue circle.

TN-12 gearbox from above. The expansion box has been removed and replaced with straight through pipes. (RK)

Chapter Six

Specialised Variants, Weapon Platforms and Development Testbeds

Specialised Variants

As soon as a new tank or AFV is introduced into service, it is usual for a range of specialised support vehicles to be developed from the chassis, being capable of keeping up with the battle tank formation, and with the commonality of spares simplifying logistics. The Chieftain was intended to be no different, but in yet another inglorious chapter of the Chieftain story, things did not quite work out as intended.

The Centurion had an almost complete family of special purpose vehicles based on it, and many of these were forced to carry on long after they were obsolete, due to the incoherent way the Chieftain programme was managed. Promising special purpose designs were cancelled because of the miserly allocation of funds by HM Treasury, successive governments leaving the Chieftain fleet and the British Army with capability gaps which were never resolved.

Chieftain ARRV Mk 7 (Iranian spec ARV) displaying at Tankfest (RK Collection)

Armoured Engineer Vehicle (Gun) and (Winch)

The Royal Engineers had been lobbying for a whole set of specialised vehicles based on the Chieftain to replace the Centurion-based vehicles then in use. Initially, three were proposed – the AEV(G), AEV(W), and the AVLB, (described below). Only the AVLB actually made it into service, so the RE had to soldier on with their increasingly antiquated Centurions.

The Armoured Engineer Vehicle (Gun) was just that, a basically standard Chieftain, fitted with a dozer blade and the famous 165 mm "Dustbin" bunker-busting gun. To apparently give it a little more

Proposed FV 4207 AEV (G). (Crown Copyright)

Proposed FV 4207 AEV (G) with 'A' frame. (Crown Copyright)

Three for the price of one – the FV 180 Combat Engineer Tractor. (Alf Van Beem, via Wikimedia Commons)

flexibility, an 'A' frame was designed to be attached to the turret. Why an 'A' frame was considered useful is anyone's guess, as it would appear to have been more of an encumbrance to the operation of the vehicle than anything else. A requirement for around fifteen vehicles was considered. The AEV (G) would have been a very useful vehicle, but in 1967 the project was killed off, and the RE had to soldier on with the Centurion into the 1990s.

The AEV(W) shared the same basic design and structure as the later ARV, including its winches and dozer blade, but with the added ability to carry and deploy a small No. 7 24 ft (7.3 m) bridge. The AEV(W) was renamed the AVRE (Armoured Vehicle Royal Engineers) in 1967, avoiding the same fate as the AEV(G), but not for long, as it in turn lost out to the FV 180 Combat Engineer Tractor and was cancelled – but not before two prototypes were up and running. Both of these prototypes were eventually reverse-engineered into "Training ARVs", whatever they were supposed to be.

ARV – Armoured Recovery Vehicle

An ARV is a vital component of any armoured formation, needed to repair and recover damaged or broken-down tanks from the battlefield or training ground. The requirement for a Chieftain ARV was issued in 1966, the design being developed by Royal Ordnance Factory Leeds. Two prototypes were eventually built during late 1970, and early 1971. The ARV was basically a Chieftain Mk 5 with the upper hull removed, replaced with a lightly armoured box-like superstructure. This had a large sloping front, replete with various storage bins required for recovery equipment. A large earth anchor/dozer blade was fitted to the front (this was not made removable, unlike the dozer blade kits for the later gun tanks). Two winches were mounted to the sloping front plate, which had a combined pull of 90,000 lbs (40.8 tonnes) with the rear vertical plate strengthened, to allow it to withstand the strain of towing a disabled tank.

On paper, this was more than capable of recovering any tank then in service. Unfortunately, this impressive sounding vehicle proved to be utterly useless when trialled by REME. The main winch failed catastrophically, prematurely ending the trial, to the relief of both the REME and factory representatives present. A specialist hydraulic engineering company, Lockheed Precision Products, was brought in to redesign all the hydraulic systems, after which the ARV proved to be an excellent vehicle. It was accepted for service in 1973, but as ROF Leeds was at full capacity building Chieftain gun tanks for the British Army and Iran, Vickers in Newcastle took over production. Deliveries did not start until 1975, finally replacing the capable, but old, slow and petrol-fuelled Centurion Mk 2 ARVs – nine years after Chieftain entered service.

Iran, as the main overseas customer for the Chieftain, also ordered the ARV, but wanted it modified to mount a five ton Atlas crane, to allow it to perform engine changes in the field, with a cradle fitted over the engine deck to carry the replacement engine. This made it a much more versatile vehicle. With the fall of the Shah of Iran in 1979, ROF and Vickers were left with a large number of completed ARVs which could not be delivered, and even more partially completed vehicles and stockpiled parts which had already been paid for. The British Army gladly accepted some of these free gifts and soon discovered that the Iranian ARV, with its winch, was a much more capable vehicle and after squeezing the money out of HM Treasury, began returning its own Mk 5 ARVs to the factory or to REME Base Workshops to be upgraded to the Iranian specification. These were designated Chieftain Mk 7 ARRV (Armoured Repair and Recovery Vehicle). The crane later proved a godsend when it was discovered the REME FV 434 Fitter's vehicle was incapable of lifting the new Challenger 1 engine pack.

The withdrawal of the Chieftain ARV fleet for conversion meant that the venerable Mk 2 Centurion ARV was brought out of war reserve stock to fill the gap, until the Chieftains were returned from works. The remaining vehicles were completed on the orders of the Government, and a considerable amount of spares did somehow get to Iran. Interestingly, Iraq also acquired fifty Chieftain ARVs, diverted from the Iranian order, supplied in a dubious arrangement (approved by the Government) via Jordan, who also purchased a large number to support its own *Khalid* and Centurion fleets. The Chieftain ARRV was deployed during the First Gulf War, but sadly proved unable to fully support the much faster Challengers in conflict conditions, leading to the crash deployment of the first three (Challenger based) CRARRVs.

AVLB – Armoured Vehicle Launching Bridge

Design work on the AVLB began in 1962, even before that of the ARV, as the result of concerted lobbying from the Royal Engineers (RE), to be part of a larger planned fleet of Chieftain-based vehicles to replace the specialised Centurion variants. The AVLB was the only one of this original family to make it into service.

The purpose-built AVLB had a special casting which extended over what would have been the turret aperture, with the mounting for the bridge launching equipment cast into it, along with the driver's and commander's hatches, creating a very strong attachment point for the extremely heavy mechanism. The original order was for 37 vehicles for the British Army, and another fourteen for Iran were added. Jordan

AVLB without its bridge which is laid out next to the vehicle. (Alan Brown)

AVLB – This folding bridge belongs to 32 Armoured Engineer Regt, BFPO 104. On return to Germany from deployment in Op Granby (1st Gulf War).(Alan Brown)

Pearson Mine Plough. In service, only ever fitted to engineer vehicles. (RK)

ordered five in the 1980s, just before Chieftain production ended. The Army then belatedly decided it needed more bridge layers, or to give it the correct military term, FV 4205 Armoured Vehicle Launching Bridge. As the Chieftain production lines had then closed, these were built by refurbishing eleven of the forty Mk 1 Chieftains, bringing them up to Mk 5/2 standard, covering the turret aperture with 19 mm plate – at the eye-watering cost of over £400,000 per vehicle. If the order had been placed twelve months earlier, they could have been built new for a fraction of that cost.

The AVLB initially used a No. 8 scissor-type bridge, which was 40 ft (12.2 m) in closed length, and when fully extended was 80 ft (24.4 m) long, covering a gap of 75 ft (22.8 m). The bridge could be launched and in place from under armour in three minutes, and recovered in ten, although this did require a crewman to dismount and link the bridge back to the launching mechanism. The No. 9 bridge was also used. This was a single span bridge, 44 ft (13.4 m) long, able to cover a gap of 40ft (12.2 m). Launch and recovery times were similar, although the No. 9 was an 'up and over' launch. Whichever bridge was used, it was an impressive sight.

Towards the end of its service life, a new range of bridges, the No. 10 (80 ft/24.5m), No. 11 (47.5 ft/14.5m) and No. 12 (39 ft/12 m) were introduced to provide tactical flexibility. The vehicle was by all accounts difficult to see out of, and scary to travel in, as when carrying the No. 8 and No. 9 bridges, it was very unstable. The AVLB was deployed in the First Gulf War in 1991, (Op *Granby*) and again on Op *Telic* in 2003 – the final deployment on Ops of the British Army Chieftain. The AVLB was often fitted with a mine plough to add more tactical flexibility.

AVRE – Armoured Vehicle Royal Engineers

The Chieftain AVRE is the tale of two distinct vehicles. The original Chieftain AVRE was developed from the previously mentioned AEV(W) proposal. Two prototypes were running and performing well by 1969, when the decision was made to abandon the AVRE in favour of the FV 180 Combat Engineer Tractor, when it became clear that funds were not available for both vehicles. (Three CETs were equivalent in price to a single AVRE.) However, the RE never forgot about their Chieftain AVRE, and when, by the 1980s, Chieftain hulls started to become available as they were replaced by Challenger, the RE proposed their own design, though without the much-loved 165 mm "Dustbin" gun (named after the shape of the bunker-busting round) to save weight, and converted in-house to save money. The vehicles had the turret removed, and the hole plated over, with a rudimentary commander's hatch placed in the centre of the vehicle. A top hamper, designed to carry up to three Class 60 roadways or three pipe fascines, was welded to the top of the hull. The front of the hamper was able to drop hydraulically to deploy the load, with a winch mounted for recovery.

The AVRE was also able to tow specialised engineer trailers, including the awesome Giant Viper mine-clearing rocket, which could be deployed and fired from under armour. The converted vehicles

AVRE carrying a fascine at the Firepower Demonstration, Land Warfare Centre, Warminster, 2005. (Graeme Main, MOD, via Wikimedia Commons)

were pampered by their crews, and each has a thin intricate figure-eight pattern of concrete anti-slip on the hull. A thin piece of checker plate was welded above the driver's compartment, as they justifiably complained about being showered with mud and dirt from the loads on the top hamper.

The original converted Chieftains became known as the "Willich AVREs" after the location of 21 RE Base Workshops, where they were converted. Captain David Clegg MBE oversaw the modification programme. In a recent Facebook posting, responding to incorrect information posted by Bovington Tank Museum (unfortunately since repeated on Wikipedia), he confirmed that seventeen were manufactured at Willich, and a further two at Wetre REME Base Workshop. These were produced for a very reasonable unit cost of £80,000, entering service in 1987.

The vehicle was a resounding success, and the decision was made in 1989 to convert more surplus Chieftains to AVREs, with the contract for an improved design going to Vickers Defence Systems in Newcastle, for a total of 48 vehicles known as CHAVREs. Each one costing a mere… (ahem) …£380,000, nearly five times the original Willich AVRE price, entering service in 1994. Sadly, it seems the MOD Procurement Executive never learned.

Fourteen of the original Willich AVREs were deployed to the Gulf in 1991, proving to be excellent and versatile vehicles. At least two of them escaped the scrapman's torch, and are now in private hands.

Weapon Platforms – (and one without)

JagdChieftain

This was a Concept Test Rig for a 1972 joint Anglo-German project to design a fixed-gun tank destroyer, of the type that had been fielded by the Germans to great effect in WWII. The gun would be able to depress and elevate, but the vehicle would have to swivel to lay onto a target. It was intended to weigh around 35 tons, and have a crew of three. The engine could be either the proven diesel of the Leopard 1, or the train wreck L60, and the main armament was also intended to be interchangeable. Service vehicles would have had the new revolutionary Chobham armour. Only one vehicle was built, fitted with a dummy gun. It has a definite presence, and was soon nicknamed *JagdChieftain*, due to its similarity to the WWII German tank destroyers. The one question that was obviously not asked at the beginning was *"Why do we need this?"*, as an ambush killer already existed in the Chieftain MBT, having all the advantages of a tank and none of the disadvantages of a tank destroyer.

Marksman SPAAG

Even when the Cold War raged at its hottest, the British Army was subject to cheese paring, salami slicing, penny pinching, and cost cutting, and sometimes, even all four at the same time! One example of this was the saga of the Chieftain Marksman Self Propelled Anti-Aircraft Gun (SPAAG). The British Army has not had a mobile anti-aircraft vehicle since the end of WWII, and still lacks this capability. The Marksman turret was developed by Marconi in the early 1980s, to provide the solution to this equipment shortfall. It was designed to be retrofitted to the existing MBT chassis, and at a stroke removed the logistical problems of introducing a new vehicle into the order of battle. The self-contained turret was designed to acquire targets out to 4 km (2.5 miles), using Marconi's own newly-developed 400 Series surveillance and tracking radar, which was designed to operate 24hrs in all weather conditions. The system would lock-on and fire within six to eight seconds of target detection, proving to be very accurate for this type of system, with a hit rate of 52.44 percent. Much better than either the German *Gepard*

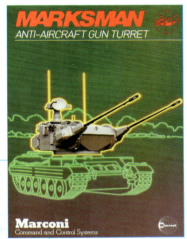

Marksman Brochure cover. (RK)

Marksman SPAAG at IWM Duxford. (Simon Ballard, via Wikimedia Commons)

or Russian ZSU 23/4 *Shilka*. The Marksman used the same 35 mm Oerlikon KDA cannon as the *Gepard*, with a rate of fire of 550 rounds per minute, although only 460 rounds were carried in the vehicle, 40 of those being anti-armour rounds. The system was designed to fire between 20 and 40 rounds per engagement. The Chieftain Marksman was trialled by the British Army in 1985, and met all requirements. The ease of installation was demonstrated when a Mk 5 Chieftain gun tank was driven into a hangar, emerging just four hours later as a fully operational Chieftain Marksman SPAAG. The Army wanted the vehicle, MOD wanted the vehicle, but HM Treasury did not want to pay for the vehicle, so the system was not adopted.

It is ironic that the only nation to purchase the Marksman, Finland, installed them on T-55 hulls, so a system designed to fight Warsaw Pact forces ended up being fitted on vehicles produced by them. The Marksman turret was also trialled on a Challenger 1 chassis, but once again, the funds to purchase the equipment were not made available. The prototype Chieftain Marksman is on display at the Imperial War Museum Duxford, and can be seen moving under its own power during special displays.

Sabre SPAAG

The Sabre was an in-house design from the Royal Ordnance Factory, which used a pair of close-coupled 30 mm cannon and Thomson CSF radar. The turret was much smaller than that of Marksman, and its ammunition load was also smaller, to the point of being inadequate, and it was overall a much inferior vehicle to the Marksman. Sabre failed to win any orders from the British Army (who had no interest in it at all) or from any overseas clients, which it was primarily designed for.

Chieftain Sabre. (Crown Copyright)

GBT 155R Self Propelled Gun

Like the Marksman, this 155 mm Self Propelled Gun turret was totally self-contained with its own internal power, and was designed to fit onto a variety of vehicles, using an adaptor ring. It was installed on both the Centurion and Chieftain, appearing at various arms exhibitions in the mid-1980s. The GBT 155R is very similar in design and appearance to the French GCT 155 mm SPG. The turret with minor modifications became the basis of the SP90 self-propelled gun project and remains in service with the British army as of 2019.

Project *Crazy Horse*

For many years, the British Army had a small fleet of "target tanks" which were used as mobile targets for Infantry anti-tank training. These were heavily up-armoured Centurions – which required drivers. Accepting the posting was considered the height of insanity, even by most drivers (who are all a little crazy anyway) and very few would willingly do it. This understandable lack of volunteers, along with the difficulties maintaining the Centurions, inspired Project *Crazy Horse* in 1987.

This was a remotely controlled Chieftain, with the gun, NBC gear, radio and ammo storage removed, and fitted with commercially available 16-channel radio control equipment, provided by Skyleader of Croydon. The controls were attached to hydraulic rams in the driver's compartment, operating

the standard driving mechanism. A colour video camera was installed in the driver's sight aperture, and the main gun removed and plated over. The fuel tank was limited to 35 litres, so if anything went wrong, it wouldn't go very far (although about five uncontrolled miles seems plenty enough!). Finally, a Red Indian Chief (meant to be Crazy Horse) was painted on the sides and front of the turret. Trials were undertaken, but the vehicle did not enter service, probably because the radio control gear was not shielded, and the tank had an alarming tendency to go crazy(!) when it picked up signals from other sources. The prototype sits gathering dust in a corner of the Bovington Tank Museum reserve collection.

Bovington Reserve Collection's precursor to Crazy Horse – the up-armoured Centurion target tank for crazy drivers. Note the deflection plates. (Phil Cater)

Lights, Camera, Inaction. Close up of Crazy Horse, awaiting restoration at the Bovington Reserve Collection. (Phil Cater)

Development Testbeds

The Aluminium Chieftain – FV 4211

By late 1969, the revolutionary Chobham, (or Burlington as it was then called) armour was ready to be trial-fitted to a tank. Initially it was intended to up-armour the standard Chieftain Mk 5/2 then in service with appliqué panels.

Three options were proposed. A partial scheme, adding 2.5 tons, a maximum protection scheme adding 3.8 tons and a close-fitting scheme, which added six tons. This project was given the code name *Almagest*. Unfortunately, even the partial scheme added too much weight for the underpowered and unreliable L60 and TN12 to handle, so in 1970, FVRDE were ordered to design and build a Chieftain hull using much lighter aluminium armour, instead of the standard Rolled Homogeneous Armour (RHA) plate. This vehicle became known as the FV 4211, or Aluminium Chieftain. This kept the weight down to 55 tons.

While the hull was new, other systems remained those of a standard Chieftain, with a minor change made to the spacing of the road wheels, to better balance the weight of the new Chobham-armoured turret. The L60 engine was also retained, although it has been suggested a rotary (Wankel-type) diesel engine then under development by Rolls-Royce was intended to replace the L60. The first hull was designed and built within thirteen months. This hull had a Windsor[1] turret fitted, ballasted to represent the weight of the proposed aluminium and Chobham turret, which had not been built at that time.

The hull completed extensive automotive trials, after which some cracking was discovered. A new improved hull was manufactured and mated with the turret, which was by then complete. Several sources claim an entirely new turret was developed, although no official confirmation can be found of this. The new No. 21 cupola, which included an Image Intensifier sight, and an experimental Advanced Integrated Fire Control System, was installed. The No. 21 cupola was not a success. Both the hull and turret were clad in Chobham armour, and side skirts were fitted, again made of sections (or 'biscuits') of Chobham armour. As the accompanying photograph shows, the FV 4211 is clearly the parent of the *Shir* 2 and Challenger.

The project was abandoned in 1972, when the decision was taken to join the Joint Future Main Battle Tank project with West Germany. In recent years, it has been claimed that nine trials vehicles were under construction at various stages of completion, some nearing troop trials, when the project was cancelled, and that the FV 4211 was intended to replace Chieftain by 1985. No official documentation has been found to confirm these claims. The completed AT 1 vehicle survives, and is held in the Bovington Tank Museum reserve collection.

---

1   A 'Windsor Turret' is a round open topped container which is loaded with lead or sandbags to bring it up to the weight of the turret it is standing in for. Due to its shape, it was once suggested it looked like the great turret at Windsor Castle, and the name stuck.

FV 4211 Aluminium Chieftain. (Crown Copyright)

The Turbine Chieftain

Gas turbines were supposed to be the next big thing in tank design – the American M1 Abrams and Russian T-80 both entered service with this type of engine. To gain experience with this type of powerplant, in the 1980s a single Mk 1 was converted to run on a Garrett GT601 gas turbine engine. The vehicle still exists, (although the turbine engine has been replaced) and can be seen at the Norfolk Tank Museum, at Forncett St Peter.

MTU Diesel engine Concept Test Rig

Another early Chieftain was converted to assess the diesel engine of the Leopard 2 built by the German MTU company, in the late 1980s. It was never intended to retro-fit the Chieftain fleet with this engine, nor was it designed to upgrade Kuwaiti Chieftains, despite rumours to the contrary. This vehicle is also still in existence, at the Yorkshire Aircraft Museum at Elvington, near York. Several offers have been made to restore the vehicle, which is in poor condition.

Chieftain 800 and 900

Chieftain 800 referred to the 1978 proposal to re-engine the Chieftain fleet with a smaller 800 bhp version of the Condor V12 engine under development for MBT 80, and later used in Challenger 1 and 2. If the Cold War had continued, there were plans to re-engine the entire Chieftain fleet with this engine, following the TOGS upgrade (Chieftain Mk 11). This would then have been renamed the Chieftain Mk 12. A deal had also been signed with the Imperial Iranian Army to re-engine their Chieftains with this engine.

Chieftain 900 was a private venture by ROF Leeds in 1981, to update Chieftain for export, using the small Condor engine uprated to 900 bhp, clad in Chobham armour bolted to the basic hull and turret – basically Chieftain in a posh frock. It was not successful and no sales were made.

Brochure for Chieftain 900. (Crown Copyright)

Chieftain 800-900. (Mercedes Babich, via Wikimedia Commons)

Chieftain 2000

GEC-Marconi had developed a new fire control system (FCS) known as Centaur, very similar to the systems now installed on most modern Western MBTs. The company approached MOD for a loan vehicle (Government Furnished Equipment) to trial it in "real world" conditions. One of the Chieftain 900 prototypes was loaned to the company in 1993, into which the new FCS was installed, and the vehicle optimistically christened Chieftain 2000. The fire control system proved effective, but no sales were made and the project shelved. The tank (without the FCS) was returned to the Government. The converted tank – actually one of the earliest Chieftains – has survived, and is now at Witham's MOD disposal sales yard at Colsterworth, Lincs.

Chieftain SID

Experiments were carried out in the 1980s aimed at reducing the noise, thermal image and radar signature of AFVs. Two Chieftains were converted, and the trials proved successful. The Chieftain SID (Signature Integration Demonstrator) was hailed as the first Stealth Tank. The design was supposed to work just like a standard tank, but the big brushes, for want of a better description, would not last ten minutes on an exercise or in action, which probably explains why they have not been seen since on an operational tank. These brushes were intended to reduce dust clouds. In order to reduce the heat signature, the engine bay was lined with gold leaf. As for the other parts of the design, they could well have been incorporated into Challenger 2, but no information can be found about this.

Chieftain SID. (Simon Q, via Wikimedia Commons)

FV 4030 Series – The evolution of Chieftain to Challenger

During the 1970s, the Shah of Iran was single-handedly keeping the British armaments industry in work, with a seemingly inexhaustible appetite for weapons, and a healthy bank balance able to pay for them. Iran was the largest export customer for the Chieftain, ordering and receiving over 900 Chieftain MBTs, and other variants based on the Chieftain chassis, over the course of the decade. However, the Iranians were unimpressed with the L60 engine and its well known reliability problems, and demanded something be done. Their list of demands amounted to a new tank. ROF Leeds proposed a staged programme of improvements, culminating in a new tank (supposedly) designed specifically to meet Iran's requirements. A contract was placed to develop the FV 4030 series of AFVs. Information of any sort on the FV 4030 programme has always been difficult to find, and is often contradictory. The full story of its development and what happened after the Iranian revolution are worthy of their own book. It would seem that successive British Governments do not want people taking a hard look at just what was going on with international arms sales in the late 1970s and throughout the 1980s...

The FV 4030/1 addressed the immediate concerns of the Iranians and was officially just a slightly upgraded Chieftain Mk 5/1. The modifications were all internal, and it is impossible to tell one of these vehicles from a standard Chieftain. The FV4030/1 had thicker belly armour for increased mine resistance, higher fuel capacity, and a modified fully automatic gearbox, to ease driver training and fatigue levels. Additional shock absorbers were fitted on the first and third bogies to improve the ride. The FV 4030/1 was shipped to Iran under the original Chieftain contract and described as a Chieftain 5/3(P). This false flagging has caused confusion on the total numbers of Chieftains built, and the numbers sold to Iran, ever since.

So why was this subterfuge undertaken? Research points to the possibility that these vehicles, or at least some of them, were in fact fitted with the 800 bhp version of the Rolls-Royce Condor engine, being developed in 1200 BHP form for the MBT 80 programme. This smaller engine fitted inside Chieftain's engine bay with minor modifications and no external changes. 191 of the FV 4030/1 or Mk 5/3(P) were delivered. A contract to update the entire Iranian fleet of Chieftains, to commence in 1985, was signed prior to the collapse of the Shah's regime in 1979. The wording on the first page of the proposal is very telling, as it states: "proposed contract for the *continued* re-engining of the Iranian Chieftain fleet..."

The second vehicle developed was the FV 4030/2 *Shir Persia* (Lion of Persia) later changed to *Shir* 1. This was to all intents and purposes a Chieftain 'cut and shut', with the front hull and turret of the

Mk 5 Chieftain, and the engine and running gear of the FV 4030/3 *Shir* 2, as the new engine was too big for the standard Chieftain engine bay. The entire rear of the new prototype *Shir* 2 was welded on to the front of the Chieftain. Only 125 of these tanks were ordered by the Iranians, as an interim version to keep the tank factories open, while they prepared for the *Shir* 2.

The suspension was upgraded to an improved version of the standard Horstmann suspension, imaginatively called "Super Horstmann", which had twice the suspension travel of the standard units, able to give a good cross-country ride and handle the considerable extra power of the new engine. This suspension is sometimes confused with the Hydrogas units of *Shir* 2/Challenger, as the road wheel spacing is almost identical.

The *Shir* 1 was also fitted with the appalling No. 84 (or Condor) Image Intensifying (II) sight. This had been MOD's preferred option to upgrade the British Army's Chieftain fleet, until they were forced to accept the privately developed TOGS, which was vastly superior. A huge amount of money had been wasted on the development of this inferior sight, and it was decided to recoup some of it by convincing the Iranians to take it as part of the FV 4030 programme, a cynical decision at best – typical of the condescending way the MOD and British armaments industry treated the countries that kept them in business. The supposedly new and advanced gunnery system on *Shir* 1 also lacked the IFCS retrofit that had been applied to all British Army and other export tanks, as this was to be included in another contract for the entire Iranian Chieftain fleet. Another example of having your cake and eating it, particularly as all other export Chieftains included IFCS.

With the cancellation of the contract by Iran's new rulers when mass production was about to start, frantic efforts were made to find an alternative buyer (although the entire order had been paid for in advance). Eventually, Jordan was convinced to take 274 of the now renamed *Khalid* MBT. Interestingly, they all had IFCS fitted as standard. Officially no *Shir* 1s were ever shipped to Iran, but unpublished photographs would seem to indicate at least two, and probably more, were in fact delivered, and remain in service, known locally as the *Mobarez* (Warrior). The *Shir* 1/*Khalid* is a good looking tank, and although it "looks the part", an Armour Trials Development Unit report written as it was about to go into production savaged it in almost all areas, declaring it to be only 18% combat ready. It is doubtful that this report was ever shown to the Iranians or Jordanians.

The culmination of this series of three vehicles was the *Shir* 2, or FV4030/3 – the "new" tank which the Iranians had been promised. It had a new Rolls-Royce diesel engine of 1200 hp developed for the proposed MBT 80 Chieftain replacement, Hydrogas suspension, which gave an incredibly smooth ride cross-country, and the revolutionary Chobham armour (the inclusion of this armour in the new tank was the major reason for the Iranian order). Its angular shape gave it the appearance of a completely new tank. In reality, the *Shir* 2 was an evolution of the Chieftain, especially where the turret and fire

FV4030/3 Shir 2 posing for a brochure photo. (Phil Cater)

control systems were concerned. The No. 84 sight was again included, this time alongside the IFCS, but the fire control system was still not up to the standards of the day.

Seven prototypes had been built and were undergoing tests at the Royal Ordnance Factory in Leeds. Mass production was scheduled to begin the following year, with long-lead items already stockpiled for the huge order of 1,225 tanks. Then the Shah was deposed in the 1979 Iranian Revolution. The British Government were informed by the new Government of Iran that all armament contracts were cancelled – not that the British would have provided the tanks to the new regime, given its stance on the revolution. At a stroke, the seemingly secure future of ROF Leeds and Vickers in Newcastle, along with much of the supporting British armaments industry, had been undermined, and over 10,000 mostly high skilled jobs placed at risk.

Concurrently, the Chieftain Replacement programme was in deep trouble. The MBT 80 was proving to be far too ambitious a vehicle. Its forecast in-service date was slipping faster than an avalanche down a mountain, with a tentative date of the mid-1990s, if not the early 2000s, and with no guarantee it would be ready even by then. Chieftain was already on the edge of perceived obsolescence, and needed to be replaced no later than the mid-1980s. Senior MOD and Army staff even considered buying a foreign tank off the shelf. So, given the choice of a working tank, admittedly not at the cutting edge in terms of gunnery, or a highly capable but paper design, yet to emerge sometime in the future, the opportunity was seized. The Government was also able to avert a political/industrial crisis, so both sides were happy.

With modifications mainly centred on the turret, which had to be reduced in size, the *Shir 2* was taken into British Army service as the FV 4030/4 Challenger, the story of which is beyond the scope of this book. But only just – what with only having improved armour and a working engine – it's really a warmed-over Chieftain – and still with those Centurion road wheels too!

Close-up of the appalling No. 84 (or Condor) Image Intensifying (II) sight. (Phil Cater)

Chapter Seven

Living with Chieftain – *The Best Job I Ever Had!*

The initial impressions of the first troopers to crew the Chieftain were how low and sleek it looked compared to the Centurion, and the fantastic noise it made. Anyone who has heard a Chieftain running at full power will never forget the awesome sound it makes – unfortunately, they also invariably notice the clouds of blue and white smoke which accompany that sound. This could give away the tank's position, and often did on exercise, when that sound and smoke gave the opposing forces time to *Prepare for Tank Action*. Chieftain was a very dirty tank compared to Centurion, or any other tank for that matter, due to the engine's chronic incontinence. Chieftain crews on exercise would often look like coal stokers from the Victorian Navy, however hard they tried to keep themselves clean (and they didn't try very hard).

Stowage was also a great problem, as no thought had been given to storing the crew's personal kit. This led to some inspired bodging (more properly known as "field modification") during its introduction into service, such as M48 tank bins liberated from range targets and other sources, mounted instead of the jerry can rack on the left side of the turret on the Mk 2. Eventually, improvements were introduced on the production lines, and from the late Mk 3/3 a commander's bin (remarkably similar to that of the M48) and an additional basket were fitted as standard on the left side of the turret. Stowage was still tight, and the Mk 10 and Mk 11 both had more rear bins welded to the back of the baskets on each side of the turret, with single jerry can racks attached to them in the gap between the bin and the NBC Pack. Mk 11s would also be seen with liberated turret baskets from the retired CVR(T) Scorpion hung from the NBC pack. The driver might also have half a long side bin attached to his splash plate, but this was uncommon. The rear long bins were used for tool storage, which the Chieftain had a con-

A major readiness inspection. 1 RTR, Tofrek Barracks, Hildesheim, 1989. The inspection was passed, but every trick in the book had been used, and some new ones invented, one crew even hanging a bag of house bricks on the breech to balance the gun to give the false impression that the gun kit was working. Supposed 100% equipment readiness was followed by a drive to Himmelsthür deployment area. On return to camp the following day, 80% breakdown rate. Absolute shambles... Happy days! (via BAOR Locations.org.)

siderable amount of due to needing both Imperial and metric sizes. All stowage bins were always kept locked, because Squaddies have no shame and would "liberate" anything not bolted down, and even some things that were.

On the Mks 10 and 11, oil can holders were fashioned from the plentiful supply of old fan belts *(see L60 chapter...)* on each side of the rear bins, and large OMD 80 and OMD 220 cans carried there, to feed Chieftain's insatiable thirst for oil.

The fuel filler caps would also leak diesel when the tank climbed a steep incline, if the fuel tanks were more than three quarters full. The fuel gauge was useless, and crews would top up whenever the opportunity arose, as the consequences of running out of fuel were dire. Charges would be brought, with the very real possibility of the commander being sacked or demoted. Unless they were an officer, who instead risked promotion even further beyond his level of competence, and posting out of the Regiment and harm's way. Avoiding these draconian penalties resulted in many thousands of gallons of fuel draining over the rear decks during the decades the Chieftain was in service.

All Chieftains could be fitted with a dozer blade, used for creating hull-down firing positions. The blade was unpopular with crews, as it took stowage space, was fragile and unreliable, caused the tank to wallow due to the extra and unbalancing weight and, being wider than the tank, made manoeuvring very difficult. Each Squadron had one tank permanently fitted with the blade. The hydraulics for the blade were housed in the front left stowage bin, further reducing space for kit. The control cables ran down the side of the tank, and into the fighting compartment via the round armoured cover on the left hand side in just before the engine compartment. The crew that usually got the short straw by having the dozer blade fitted to their tank was the Squadron Second in Command's crew (2IC), call sign 0C (*Zero Charlie*), the Officer Commanding (OC) being *Zero Bravo*.

Some Regiments from the late 1980s onwards, including 1 RTR, fitted a loudspeaker to the side of the dozer tanks above mounted above the external antenna box on the side of the turret, using the old Larkspur radio mount and connected to civilian boom boxes that had become available around that time. Most tanks had them wired into the intercom system too, and were given the official sounding name of *On Tank Stereos*, or the more military sounding 'OTS'. Particular care had to be taken to turn them off when transmitting on the Squadron or Regimental nets. They were used to play extremely loud music, carefully chosen for added shock effect, such as AC/DC's *Hell's Bells*, then *Back in Black* (in tribute to the RTR). Especially effective on Squadron attack runs against Infantry on exercises was Wagner's *Ride of the Valkyries*, followed by Black Sabbath's *War Pigs*. But if in a particularly good mood, the Squaddie's universal favourite, the sound track from the *Blues Brothers* movie, would be played at maximum volume.

When in barracks, that is to say, most of the time, the Chieftain would not have any camouflage nets on it and was kept as clean as possible, due to the pride of the crews and the usual Army makework.

However, on exercise, camouflage netting became increasingly important over the Chieftain's lifetime. This was stowed in many different ways – it is almost possible to tell the year a photo was taken by the stowage of the cam nets (and the moustaches of the crew, very popular in the 1970s!). Certain Regiments can also be identified by the way they hung the nets. Some would store them in the baskets on either side of the turret, others had them twisted up and laid across the turret, where the casting was joined to the rest of the turret, and tucked down the sides of the TUAAM (Tuning Unit Automatic Antenna Matching) box and searchlight/TOGs barbette. Other nets would be laid across the front of the tank, between the front bins and the splash guard. Another popular method in the 1970s was to string the nets down the sides of the bazooka plates, but this made them easy to tear off when going cross-country. "Camming up" was second nature to tank crews on exercise, and done automatically when pulling into an overnight or tactical position.

Experienced crews "acquired" sheets of shiny and slippery brown hessian, which were cut to size and placed under the cam net, then rolled up. This made the job of covering a tank quick and easy, as the heavy net wouldn't catch on every twig or obstacle on the tank and in the trees. Repeated use made the nets look ratty and worn, which actually helped the net blend into its surroundings better. The gun was almost always wrapped in a net on exercise to help disguise the long length of the gun barrel. To allow the Muzzle Reference System a clear line of sight, this would be removed during the range firing period, which usually took place straight after a field exercise, while the other nets and exercise equipment usually remained in place.

Early Chieftains used the Larkspur radio, but from 1979 these were replaced by Clansman, which remained with the Chieftain for the rest of its service life. Clansman was a generally robust system and easy to use, built to withstand hard use – "*Squaddie proof*". However, it did not like very hot temperatures, and would go unserviceable faster than you could say "*radio check*" if not kept cool. Needless to say, the REME radio techs did not like hot weather. Standard fit was two radios, one for the Squadron net and one for Regimental. The commander would hear Squadron radio traffic in one ear, Regimental in the other, and the crew intercom in both.

Command tanks had more radios, so even more work for the loader, who would often act as commander when the OC or 2IC was outside of their tank – as they were a considerable amount of the time. Overnight radio watches were very boring and monotonous, but sometimes assistance to stay awake came from an unexpected source. The Russians would often transmit the day's radio chatter, which they had recorded, back over the operational frequencies, and sometimes score and helpfully comment on the quality of the operators and procedures. Answering back was obviously strictly forbidden. The Russians would also try and spoof units into taking false commands and changes of orders during exercises. They had some very good mimics who could impersonate particular officers. Standard procedure was to challenge any order with the word "*Authenticate*" and use the code system in use at the time to

confirm it was the real officer or HQ. Mistakes did happen, and the Russians had some success – the gullible offender found themselves in trouble so deep they needed a straw to breathe! In officer parlance: *"Interview Without Coffee."*

When the Russians were not providing entertainment, boredom got the best of some on radio watch, and they would break radio silence or click the transmit button to see if they could get a return click. The net sometimes sounded like a swarm of angry crickets, until an officer or senior NCO broke in and stopped it. The most famous exchange, enshrined in BAOR history, is as follows:

"God, I'm bored!"

Incensed Regimental Sergeant Major: *"Call sign, identify yourself!!!!"*

"I said I'm bored, not stupid!"

The culprit was never caught, but kept people laughing for years to come. Perhaps he was a Russian?

Working on and living with the Chieftain was not all good fun and, excluding the engine, its worst shortcoming by far was the lack of a heater, which had been deleted during development – to save weight. This failing was never corrected, despite repeated requests from the Regiments equipped with Chieftain. One reason actually given was *"it is not cold enough in the BAOR Region of Operations to justify the cost of installation of a heater"*, something crews on watch at Zero Three Hundred Hours Zulu on the Soltau training area in the depths of winter, (or worse still, Med Man 7 in BATUS) with ice on the inside of the tank, would violently disagree with. (Recall that even the ammunition containers were lined with anti-freeze!) The lack of a heater caused untold misery for the crews, and reduced the efficiency of the tank, as nothing slows down a crew and destroys morale faster than the cold. If the tank was in a non-tactical environment, then the gun could be traversed over the back decks, elevated, and a half-shelter thrown over, to create a tent for the crew who would lay their sleeping bags on the hopefully still warm engine decks.

The Crew

Drivers had it good on Chieftain, compared to the Centurion. It was much easier to drive, as it had a semi-automatic as opposed to manual gearbox although, as previously mentioned, achieving smooth changes was always an art form, requiring considerable skill, almost impossible for inexperienced or just plain bad drivers to achieve. If he was annoyed with his travelling companions, he would often deliberately mess up a gear change, causing the tank to lurch forward or backwards, with the malign intent that the turret crew would bash their heads against one of the many protrusions in the interior. If successful, it was not unknown for the commander to then climb down the outside of the turret, and kick the errant driver in the head a few times. These repeated kicks soon convinced even the most stubborn of drivers of the error of their ways.

Fortunately, the Army decided that the number of unexplained head injuries incurred by tank crews was becoming unacceptable, and introduced the "bonedome" crew helmet into use in the early 1970s.

A Mk 9 showing the amount of kit and cam nets carried on exercise. 1 RTR pre-BATUS training, Soltau, 1988. (H. Robinson)

This medieval torture device was universally hated by all who had to wear it, as it was close fitting, and felt like it was crushing their skull. The introduction of Clansman radios, and the new helmet required for its headsets, finally freed tank crews from the most tenacious grasp of this evil invention. Of course, the bean-counters then had a pile of useless helmets, which they managed to palm off onto the Iranians (probably at an inflated price too!). Both of these helmets did, however, do their job, and prevent the previously commonplace head injuries resulting from being thrown into the many projections inside the tank, and from the occasional corrective kick as well.

The driver's reclining seat was the best bed on the tank, so comfortable in fact they could fall asleep while driving, only to be rudely awoken by the rest of the crew screaming at them when a turn was missed. Perhaps they were worse for wear too, as the additional projectile racks on either side of the driver were ideal for holding tins of lager. The sound of a tinny being cracked open upon daybreak would often signal to the rest of the crew that the driver was awake. Drivers, or *Cab Rats* as they were known, pretty much lived on the hideous McEwan's red lager when on exercise. To this day, it is not known how many AF B252 Charge Sheets were drawn up, citing *Conduct to the Prejudice of Good Order and Military Discipline, in that Trooper [...] at [...] on [...] was found to be Drunk in Charge of a Chieftain, contrary to Section 69 of the Army Act, 1955*. Still, they had to catch you first...

In contrast to the rough improvisation among the rank and file tanks, it was rumoured, though never confirmed, that some Cavalry Regiment Officer's tanks were suitably modified to meet their own more exacting requirements. White wines (and a strong cheese selection) were cooled in an insulated ammo bin, while red wines and a single bottle of port would be carefully stored in a custom-built wire-framed wine rack located above the turret ring (being at the required room temperature there). While far more practical, boxed wine would have been considered a most severe *faux pas*, though disposable plastic wine glasses may have been grudgingly tolerated, being the most practical solution when deployed on manoeuvres.

It was inevitable that Army life, and Chieftain in particular, would lead many astray to the demon drink, be that out in the field, or in the 'Fallingbarstool' Mess. It was a hideously complex piece of machinery, and the maintenance schedule was very intensive and monotonous, whether in barracks, or while deployed out in the filthy and muddy countryside.

On exercise, you never knew when a tank would decide to throw its toys out of the pram and break, in one or more of the many interesting and varied ways which it could. The most 'interesting' of all being engine 'runaways', in which uncontrolled fuel leaks within the engine innards met the combustion

The Worst Jobs I Ever Had...

Chieftain had two particularly difficult tasks – Track Bashing and changing the springs on the suspension units. The former was hard graft, and the latter was downright dangerous.

Tracks were constantly monitored and tightened as required, using the idler sprocket adjuster, and a very long bar, which required at least two men to move it. The track was also known to throw its rubber pads, and the track pins had to be regularly checked to ensure the securing circlip was in place. The round holes on each piece of track elongated over time, becoming almost rectangular. When the track sag could no longer be tensioned by adjusting the idler wheel, there was no other option than to break the track, and remove a track link or two. When the track was down from 97 to 94 links, the entire track had to be replaced. New track came in six or ten link sets,which had to be joined together using a sledgehammer to drive the pins through to make up the required 97 links. It was always better to do this prior to an exercise on a nice flat and clean tank park, with lots of tea available, rather than in some muddy German field in the rain (and it always rained when changing tracks). If the tank threw a track on exercise, the work involved in track bashing could and did break the spirit of even the most fanatical optimist.

Wherever track bashing was done it was hard, heavy, backbreaking and demoralising work. It certainly led to the litany of bad backs, busted knees and arthritis which all former tank crews complain of. Describing the process in any greater detail would be mind numbingly boring, and far too depressing. To this day, the author still hates assembling even model kit tracks.

Changing the spring packs was worse still. The Horstmann suspension units gave little trouble during Chieftain's service, but every part requires replacing at some point, and when it came down to changing the spring packs, drivers felt like they were playing Russian roulette, as you never knew what would happen. The spring was under tremendous tension, and there was no room to fit spring compressors, so the tension had to be wound off very, very slowly, one thread at a time, while hoping that when the thread did let go, the spring tension had been sufficiently relaxed. If not, then the spring could severely injure the unfortunate tasked with changing it, or anyone else unlucky enough to be in its way as it made its break for freedom. One crewman lost his thumb, and there are many stories of other gruesome injuries. During one spring change, as the last thread of the locking plate bolt was released, the spring flew thirty feet across a hangar, through a brick wall, into the troop stores, and then ricocheted up and out through the hangar roof. It was a miracle no-one was injured or killed.

On reflection, there were more onerous tasks. The third worst job was *Ammo Bashing* – the sight of the ammunition lorries arriving at the range would have anyone not gainfully employed scattering to the four winds. But few escaped being press-ganged into unloading the unfeasibly heavy brown steel cases. First, removing the packaging, which all had to be stacked neatly to be reused, and then breaking down pallets before re-stacking the ammunition. Then hauling all the heavy ammo up to the tanks. Passing each load up to the gunners and loaders to store inside, before going back and getting another round or bag charge, and doing it all again! And all this whatever the weather. Even worse, the poor sods doing the ammo bashing were usually the drivers and other "spare" crewmen, who didn't even get the fun of firing the rounds downrange!

Now, the fourth worst job... no, must stop right here – before this book ends up as two volumes.

RK

Track pin being hammered home after removing a link. (H Robinson)

Trackbashing on a Mk 11 in Canada. Rope is beng pulled across the drive sprocket to lift the track onto the idler wheel. (RK)

Horstmann suspension unit. (Phil Cater)

Ammo Bashing. In uncommonly decent weather. (RK Collection)

chamber. The clue was in the name – when that happened, we would all scarper. Having legged it to a (hopefully) safe distance, it was a most unforgettable scene. The noise as the engine wound itself up to destruction was amazing – imagine a Spitfire in a terminal full power dive, and then double it. When the inevitable end came, it was spectacular, often ejecting various small and large parts of the engine through the decks, into what seemed like low earth orbit. One such runaway occurred when a rebuilt engine was being run up at an REME Base Workshop, resulting in a fire which destroyed most of the workshop complex.

You could, however, guarantee that whatever did break, be that some minor component or the entire engine, it would always involve vast quantities of dirty fluids, which had to be cleaned up first. Of course, the driver was the one who got to help with the frequent engine changes. Many became very proficient at prepping the L60 pack for lift before the REME had even arrived on site, which saved a great deal of time, but despite this, an engine change was never quick or easy.

The basic checks on the vehicle, known as 'first and last parade', ensured the driver was the dirtiest member of the crew on exercise, or in barracks. The longer they stayed in the job, gaining more experience, the better able they were to spot faults developing and prevent them. They learned many tips and tricks, and some (frankly inspired) bodges to keep a Chieftain running. So most of them being a little crazy probably helped. One such inspired bodge was an improvised gear change, following failure of the driver's foot pedal linkage. The crew were asked for their ID "dog tag" chains. These were then linked together, and the long chain hooked to the emergency gear change solenoid in the engine bay. As the driver called for a change on the intercom, the commander yanked the chain, and the tank was able to get back to base.

The Gunner had the most confined seat, down in the depths of the turret. If you suffered from claustrophobia, you weren't going to last long. The seat was also very uncomfortable, with the commander's boots in his back most of the time, and large, very heavy and potentially very lethal pieces of metal swinging away in front, and to his side. During exercises, gunners had the least to do of all the crew and, apart from turning on the gun kit at the start of the day, they could spend entire exercises huddled in their sleeping bags, trying to stay warm. Gunners would often help drivers with their tasks, out of sheer boredom.

The gunner's position was very confined and any loose clothing or kit was easily trapped by either the breech, or even worse, the turntable (turret floor which rotated with the turret) and the side of the tank, which would then try and pull the unfortunate gunner into the innards of the tank. A carelessly placed boot could be, and sadly quite often was, trapped and crushed between the turntable and the side of the tank. Likewise, loaders who stood on a so-called safety bar when standing in their hatch could also very easily slip and their leg become trapped in the same gap, causing at best a severely bruised leg and at worst bones shattered in multiple places, a potentially life threatening injury. This was called, with typical Squaddie gallows humour, "*being eaten by the turret monster.*" Such cautionary tales of these frequent and often horrific accidents were used to reinforce the importance of always being vigilant and never becoming complacent.

Another danger, and the way you could often tell a *NIG* gunner (all new crew straight from training were nicknamed NIGs, for New In Germany) on his first exercise by the black eyes and swollen or broken nose, caused by looking through the 'AutoStab' gunsight while on the move. The sight was linked to the stabilised gun, and would swing with great force back and forth, as the tank careered along uneven ground, something recruits were not exposed to in training.

It could be said the gunner's lot was not a happy one! Even when in barracks, he couldn't expect an easy time. Before the annual range firing – something every Regiment in the Royal Armoured Corps wanted to excel at – the gunner, along with the commander and loader, would be trained mercilessly on the simulators, by the dreaded Gunnery Instructor, or more (in)correctly, *Instructor, Gunnery* (IG). If you can imagine all the worst stereotypical Drill Sergeants in history rolled into one, then double it, you might have an inkling of how evil they could be, all in the pursuit of the mythical "three in the air" at once. During gunnery training, the sight of the turret crews, and gunners in particular, running around the tank park holding GPMGs above their heads while chanting whatever it was (that they must never do again), was very common. A GPMG held high becomes very heavy, very quickly! These unconventional motivational methods were nevertheless quite effective, and British gunnery was, and is, unsurpassed by any other nation, proven in the First Gulf War in 1991.

During the annual range firing, individual crews would compete for the best score on a battle run down the range, so any mistake – or God forbid, a target missed by the gunner – would result in a swift kick to the back of his head from the commander, being ideally placed for such corrective action, perched as he was above the hapless gunner.

On one memorable occasion, the author saw a 'NIG' gunner literally thrown from the turret by the incensed commander, after he took over a minute to fire only to bounce the round off the ground 100 metres in front of the tank. With the passenger disembarked, the tank then proceeded to complete the battle run, with the commander acting as the gunner. The unfortunate gunner was then relegated to standing guard for the remaining week of the ranges, and later Returned to Unit for remedial training.

Chieftains on Soltau training area moonscape – note the clouds of blue smoke. (RK)

The Loader was the hardest working member of the crew, almost constantly in motion, having to monitor the radios, take down and decode messages, checking for clearance as the tank moved on roads or cross-country (the loader and commander each took a side). During the range firing period, the loader moved so fast, he was a blur – loading the main armament with the required ammunition, pulling rounds from difficult to reach places in the turret, loading the co-ax, clearing the many jams that occurred due to kinked belts and full spent round bags, as well as feeding the commander's GPMG with new 200 round boxes. The actual actions required to do each of these things have been covered in other books on the Chieftain, but none explain the speed and urgency with which they were required to be done, all within an exceptionally tight space inside the turret.

The loader had to keep that up all day, and complete his other tasks as well. If some minor miracle occurred and he was able to momentarily relax, he had a folding jump seat. But no-one wants to remain inside a noisy, dirty and smelly turret unless they really have to. All loaders would relish the chance to stand with their hatch open, to practice posing, while dreaming of the joyous day upon which they would be promoted to Tank Commander. Once a loader succeeded in that lofty ambition (not all did) they found that job to be much easier and definitely less physically demanding, although very few commanders will admit it.

Probably the most important job of the loader, the one upon which his future illustrious career depended, was to keep the BV (Boiling Vessel) full and boiling, to provide hot tea or coffee on demand and warm the rations if an overnight camp was unscheduled. Putting an already opened tin of pilchards into the BV was something one loader never lived down! Experienced crews would bribe the REME electrician to make up a set of extension leads for the BV, so it could still be used when live firing was taking place (the BV was mounted at the rear of the turret, and when the main gun recoiled from firing, it completely filled that space).

Even this simple sounding task could be highly dangerous in the tight confines of the turret. If a loader slipped when passing a cup of tea to the gunner or commander while travelling cross-country and fell over the breech, he risked being crushed to death by a bump in the terrain causing the breech to suddenly swing up to the turret roof when the AutoStab (automatic stabilisation system) was engaged – which it almost always was. One Chieftain had a tin mug crushed into the turret roof by just such an incident. Thankfully, the loader was able to roll off the breech just moments before. The mug was left embedded in place, serving as a stark reminder of the ever-present dangers.

An Instructor once gave a salutary warning during a lecture to new recruits to the Royal Armoured Corps – *"Tanks are designed to kill people – and they don't care if it's you, or the enemy."*

D Sqn 1 RTR Himmelstur crash out area, 1989. Never mind the outbreak of morale – note all the additional stowage on the Mk 11 compared to the original Mk 2. (RK)

The Commander would have worked his way up through the ranks to at least Corporal, and have attended a six month specialised training course. While having a thorough knowledge of all the crew roles, both through personal experience and the Commander's Course, he would have originally specialised in either the automotive or gunnery systems on the tank. He was responsible for anything that went wrong, taking on the added responsibility of signing for the tank and all its kit, and could – believe it or not – have the cost of any missing kit deducted from his modest wage. Needless to say, some became more than slightly paranoid on this point. The commander was also in charge of map reading, fighting the tank, and most importantly (having long practiced way back when he was a mere loader), posing outside the commander's hatch on road runs, or at any other time he could get away with it.

Officers, or *Ruperts* in Army slang, of course did not learn this way and were placed in command of a troop of tanks, merely by dint of their Rank, regardless of actual ability. Some actually turned out OK – given time – while others remained downright dangerous. None could read a map. Their sad lack of knowledge regarding the vehicle they commanded was (sometimes) rectified by teaming them with an experienced NCO who was ready to be promoted to command a tank of their very own. However, cooking duties would be shared by the crew, always excluding officers, who were considered far too clueless to be let loose with a gas stove, never mind a map or radio!

A veteran crew would have a crew fund, which everyone paid into, used to purchase civilian camping stoves and utensils, as well as stashes of spices and civilian foods, to improve the standard issue Compo rations. These were universally loathed, with nicknames such as *Chicken in a Dead Horse* (chicken in black bean sauce) and *Cheese, Possessed* (processed cheese) – which was inedible, but extremely useful for plugging leaks in the engine cooling system – basically, organic rad weld! The boiled sweets and chocolate were nice, often the choccy bars would be printed in 'foreign' (usually Arabic, and not quite out of date; the Army was always looking for a bargain). Compo rations also left you constipated, which was useful, as you only got three pieces of loo paper per crewman. As the expression went, *one up, one down, one polish!* The Compo was still better than the American MRE – US troops would often trade anything for British Compo, much to the Squaddie's bemusement.

The Chieftain itself was adapted in ways the designers never envisioned. To improve the crew's lives on exercise, the central bazooka plate (side skirt) could be lowered to horizontal, making an ideal dining

Extracting *The Flask*

The Gun Control Equipment and three-part ammunition had its faults, but was generally reliable. It did, on occasion, fail, so various drills had been established for whenever this happened. If the gun misfired, then the call "MISFIRE – WAIT THIRTY" would go out. The crew waited for the specified period, and then manually remove the vent tubes (which triggered the bag charge) and opened the breech to very carefully extract it. The usual reasons for a misfire were faulty vent tubes, or a dud charge. But, if it was damp, the bag charge could also slow burn – before firing.

One famous character from 1 RTR, known as *The Flask*, as he loved his tea, always carried a flask of tea and still always had a brew on nearby too. He was acting as loader when the gun misfired. Never one to miss an opportunity for a brew, he stepped behind the breech, and put the BV back in place to boil the water. He had just stepped back to the side when the gun fired, flattening the BV to less than an inch thick, spraying warm water around the turret.

The Flask, realising how close to death he had just been, fainted dead away, and so the crew then got to practice the turret casualty evacuation procedure. Incidentally, they discovered the epaulets on the modern coveralls were not as strong as the earlier pattern, as they ripped straight off as they tried to lift him out of the loader's hatch, dropping him back into the turret. (Nobody thought to use the spare extra-strong fan belt as an improvised sling.) The rest of the Squadron, upon discovering what was going on, helpfully fell about laughing.

The Flask was later presented with the flattened BV, mounted on a plaque, to commemorate the occasion. He was a true Regimental character, and a very thick pamphlet could be written about his exploits in 1 RTR!

table for the preparation of the aforementioned meals. A petrol cooker was issued, but was pretty lethal to use, and most crews used their own civilian camping stoves. As mentioned, the insulated bag charge bins were ideal for storing cans of lager and bottles of spirits, vital provisions to sustain crew morale, and they kept the drinks cool as well. Cornflakes with Baileys instead of milk for breakfast was not uncommon, and most delicious. Most main meals seemed to be some sort of curry, or as it was called, a "*Scouse Lob*", with everything thrown in and mixed up.

If you couldn't face another Compo meal, and were based in West Germany, then the name Wolfgang would be familiar to you. Wolfgang, "*Legend of Soltau*", as he is now known, would travel the length and breadth of the exercise area in his bright blue Mercedes van, emblazoned with "*Wolfgang's Grill Shop*" and "*Wittinger Pils*", dispensing *Bratty mit Pommes und Currywurst, Frikadellas,* and coffee which could keep you awake all week, and many other goodies. All for cash, or on tick (credit), but God help you if you didn't pay up at the end of the exercise! Wolfgang was also famous for knowing where

Essential crew supplies. Coke for the coke dispenser and the foul Tennants lager for the driver. (RK Collection)

Accidents will Happen – No Matter How Prepared You Are!

The legendary Harry 'H' Robinson is famous for being in every photo ever taken of 1 RTR (or so it seems). He very kindly sent some photos – along with the following account of an unfortunate incident – and the barrel cleaning afterwards. Note how his naughty tank was exiled from the rest of the Squadron. The photo of him standing on the barrel is included to further the myth of 'H' appearing in every publication!

No previous work on Chieftain has ever mentioned that despite all the technology employed, when closed down, the visibility through the various sights was absolutely appalling…

Barrel buried up to fume extractor, after falling into unseen hole. The tank came to a sudden stop! (H Robinson)

This incident took place on Soltau, probably 1988-ish, during 1 RTR pre – BATUS training. The crew consisted of me (then a Sergeant) as the Commander, Mick Donnelan, the Loader, Stevie Barrett, the Gunner and Swatteridge, the Driver. It was near the Tank Bridge on Soltau, fully closed down, and we went into a huge hole which resulted in the barrel digging into the ground up to the fume extractor.

Donny was taken off the exercise with a badly damaged arm and shoulder, having been caught between the turret roof and the breech (he was lucky it wasn't worse). The tank was pulled out backwards by the ARRV and the barrel given a quick check by the REME Armourer and given the all clear, but it took some cleaning! I believe it then had a full REME inspection when we returned to Hildesheim, again, all OK.

WO2 (SSM) (Retired) Harry "H" Robinson

Aiming for Australia. (H Robinson)

Because every book or photo that mentions 1 RTR has to have H Robbo included! (H Robinson)

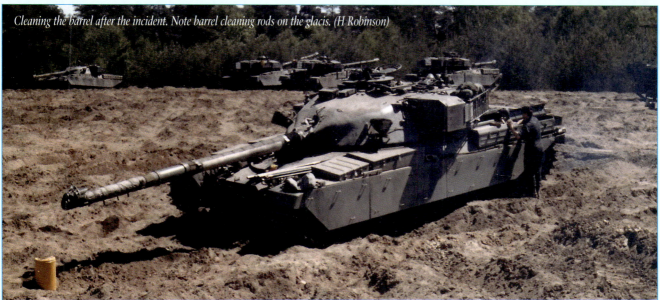

Cleaning the barrel after the incident. Note barrel cleaning rods on the glacis. (H Robinson)

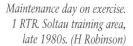

you would be before you did, and would be waiting for you in the hide, sending the Squadron Sergeant Major into apoplectic fits of rage if you were pretending to be tactical. Wolfgang helped many a lost tank crew to find where they were supposed to be – the embarrassment of being led in to your overnight halt, to the jeers of the other crews, was a small price to pay. (They made you pay a beer fine too!) You could pay Wolfgang to wait five minutes and arrive after you, but nobody ever fell for that. The amazing cross-country abilities of his various civilian Mercedes vans were never explained, but Wolfgang could teach today's so-called *mud pluggers* a thing or two!

'Squadron Smokers' – barbeques – were something everyone looked forward to over weekends and public holidays, when the Germans declared vehicle movement *streng verboten*. Vast quantities of food and beer were consumed around a large fire pit. Needless to say, things did occasionally get a little out

Maintenance in the field – not a Happy Bunny! (Neil Carter)

"We have a full tank of gas, half a pack of cigarettes, it's dark and we're wearing sunglasses!" (RK Collection)

of hand, such as on the most unfortunate occasion when the cooks went and picked the wrong kind of mushrooms in the woods for that evening's curry, leading to the entire squadron being stoned out of their minds – 126 highly trained professionals rendered quite useless for several days afterwards. (This being the only instance of a Mushroom Story appearing in a Mushroom Book! *To date.... Editor*)

There are no photos of Squadron Smokers, for two reasons: 1. Officially, they never happened; 2. What happens on Soltau stays on Soltau. Or did until now. A Squadron smoker was most definitely not your dinky back garden BBQ, the hidden fire pit resembled a WWII bomb crater, and was several feet across and deeper than the tallest squaddie. The point being, this was one huge abyss. Before the aforementioned mushrooms had begun to take effect, but after the alcohol was causing a good buzz all

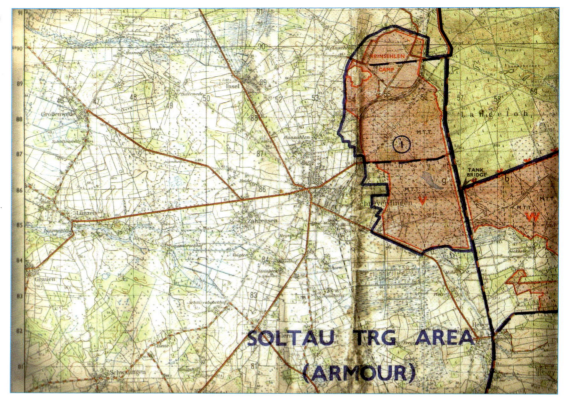

Soltau training area (RK)

SOLTAU TRG AREA (ARMOUR)

The bazooka plate breakfast bar. (RK Collection)

round, it was seen that the fire was dying down. Some genius then decided to that pouring OEM 220 oil into the pit would reinvigorate it, but then decided/discovered it was too awkward to carry to the fire pit, so lobbed the entire barrel from a turret bin straight onto the fire pit. The instant conflagration as the superheated drum exploded set fire to some of the slower moving soirée attendees, and to several nearby trees. Luckily, the tanks had hand-held CO_2 fire extinguishers, and these were used by the more sober partygoers to limit the damage to the trees at the chaotic scene. The blazing troopers were put out by tripping them as they carered around and rolling them in the dirt, not that you could tell given the generally filthy condition of a Chieftain crewman on exercise! Soon after the panic had subsided over, the mysterious hallucinations and strange dancing began.

After the deleterious effects of the mushrooms had finally worn off, a few days later sterling, and effective efforts were then made to hide the scorch marks on the trees, by throwing mud at them. As Squadron Smokers never happened, the German Environmental Inspection Officers (*Die Umweltaufsichtsbehörden*) never found out.

The Tankie's Guide to the Chieftain

Field Exercises, while the highlight of the training year, could still be very monotonous, and the crew had to find various distractions to amuse themselves.

There is a square armoured box on the left rear of the Chieftain, next to the main exhaust, with a handle on the underside. This is, in fact, the *Tank Infantry Telephone*, or TIT (*Yes, really!*). If some brave soul used this phone, it cut into the crew intercom system at very high volume, creating much irritation and deafness within. So the very first thing any newly qualified driver was taught when arriving at their Regiment was to rev the engine as high as possible in such instances. A face full of Chieftain exhaust smoke, combined with the screaming noise of an L60 very close up, soon taught the Infantry to never, ever, use this phone.

By the time the Mk 10 and 11 were in service, most of the phones were broken or disconnected, so new ways of having fun with the Infantry had to be devised. Some bright spark (*but how?!*) discovered that you could fit three cans of Coke (or any other carbonated beverage of your choice) into the space previously occupied by the handset. So, when stopped near Infantry, Crewman A would walk round, pull the handle and get a Coke, closely followed by Crewman B doing the same. Finally Crewman C (carefully auditioned for his deadpan acting skill), would wander round, grab the last Coke, and 'notice' the incredulous Infantrymen, and exclaim something convincing, such as

"Oh, didn't you know it had a drinks dispenser? Help yourselves!"

Whereupon, the crews all round would fall about laughing as the hapless Squaddie tried to get the dispenser to work. In turn, in BATUS, the Infantry would hose tanks down with live ammunition, riddling the crew's maggots (sleeping bags) and kit, although if you got the wrong OC the retaliation from the tank could be seriously over the top – but that's another story. (The *Battle Run* sequence provides a clue!)

Very late in the research of this book, Bovington Tank Museum Workshop Technician Johnathon Kneebone (ex 3 RTR), began exchanging stories during a visit to the Chieftains in the Reserve Collection, a couple of which are repeated here.

Apparently the searchlight on the turret side was often claimed to be the Crew Washing Machine (or more correctly in Army parlance, Washing Machine (Crew)) when showing Infantry or other Arms round the tank. (The author, being from the TOGS generation, was unaware of this particular wind-up). Given the aforementioned usual filthy state of the crew, it shows how gullible some Infantry were – it's no wonder we called them 'Grunts'.

On another occasion, when a gearbox had been removed, but the replacement not yet fitted, the opportunity to wind up some other impressionable young infantry was grasped, when they were informed that a spare crewman was always carried. Lo and behold, a *Man in Black* would then be revealed, resting in his sleeping bag, nonchalantly reading his newspaper.

The Infantry exclaimed: *"Isn't it loud in there, mate?"*

To which, Spare Crewman replied: *"Eh? What did you say?"* and this went back and forth, until the 'Grunts' realised they were being had...

A selection of the delectable (horrific and almost inedible) compo rations issued to tank crews, mind you the boiled sweets and sausages were nice! (RK Collection)

The beloved Boiling Vessel. (RK Collection)

The hated bone dome – God knows why he's smiling... (H Robinson)

Typically filthy crew in front of a Dozer blade equipped Chieftain. (RK)

Wolfgang, the Legend of Soltau. (RK)

Even Wolfgang sometimes got stuck on the Soltau moonscape. (RK Collection)

Chapter Eight

Moving with Chieftain

Chieftain was an easy tank to drive, but to drive it well took real skill, something not all drivers had, and some of the tasks required of them were both dangerous and frightening, in equal measure.

Almost all movement of the Chieftain during its service was operational or tactical, as the Army never deployed it at strategic distance. The BATUS tanks were shipped by sea (via commercial carriers, or Royal Fleet Auxiliaries). Operational movement would preferably be by rail, or tank transporter, and only short road distances were undertaken using the tanks. Track miles were carefully monitored and very sparingly allocated. BAOR covered a wide expanse of northern Germany, with large distances between bases, depots and exercise areas. Moves by rail or road would be more economical and practical, though requiring planning in great detail over several weeks beforehand.

Tanks have been moved by train since their invention, and the Army is adept at this style of movement. It is in fact, the restrictions of the British/European rail gauge and tunnels which defines the maximum width, height and length of all Western tanks. (Notably, the reduction in turret size between the *Shir* 2 and Challenger 1 was dictated by rail tunnel dimensions.)

During the Cold War, the *Bundesbahn* (West German Railways) was still using the same freight rolling stock as its predecessor, the *Reichsbahn*. Their flatbed wagons, while suitable for Panthers or Panzer IVs, were marginal for Chieftain, which exceeded the wagon width by a few inches each side. The roadwheels matched the width of the flatbed, while the outer track would overhang.

On arrival at the loading siding, an officious West German with a tape measure, in a uniform almost identical to his wartime predecessor (eagles omitted!) would be waiting. Above all, especially if you were *New In Germany*, with the ink still wet on your Driver (Chieftain) Specialist Qualification, you did not want to be first on, with a seemingly endless line of empty and over-narrow flatcars stretching ahead into infinity. All of which had to be driven over, and worse still, reversed off again, at journey's end.

4th/7th Dragoon Guards, Detmold, 1987. (David Gillespie) This was achieved by following the directions of your marshalling guide, who would raise one arm or the other to correct left or right. They would use torches at night, whenever some lunatic Officer had decided it would be a good idea to practice loading under tactical conditions (i.e., no lights).

Pull just a fraction too hard on the sticks, and the tank would slide off the side of the wagon, halting the loading until a crane could be brought in. Until the next unfortunate driver tipped theirs over the edge, you then became the most despised man in the Squadron or Regiment, with the wrath of the SSM, RSM, OC, and CO all directed your way, in rapid succession. Sometimes, the railwaymen would forget to lower the stabilising jacks during loading, and then, the whole wagon would tip, and the tank would slide off. Whereupon, the wrath of the Higher Paid Help would then be equally shared between the Germans and the hapless driver – rather unfair for the driver – but such is (Army) life. The accompanying photo of the tank with the red square is one such example of this type of mishap.

After bumping over several narrow wagons to finally alight on your own, Herr Massbandmann (Mr Tape Measure Guy) would appear, absentmindedly click his heels upon greeting the Squadron Sergeant Major, and then carefully check both sides of each tank's alignment with his micrometer. If *Alles* wasn't in *Ordung*, you would then spend as long as it took, rocking back and forth to make minute adjustments, doing the Rail Wagon Shuffle, until he was completely satisfied. Meanwhile, the increasingly red-faced SSM looked on, and frequently at his watch, too. glowering as his lovingly crafted loading schedule, meticulously drawn up over several preceding weeks, and all marked with highlighters in several pretty colours, disappeared down the plughole. Slowly.

Once Herr Massbandmann was content with every tank positioning, there was yet more toil to be done – chaining the tank up, hammering in the chocks to the wooden bed, and securing everything down, to await his final inspection, and declaration that *Alles* was now in *Ordung*. Only then could you escape to the Third Class coach, laden with personal kit, yellow handbags[1] and the GPMGs from the tank. Settled in with compo rations and a flask of tea, to be carefully eked out over many hours of very slow travel. You could even be shunted into sidings, most definitely not being considered as priority freight by the *Bundesbahn*. Then you had to do it all again on arrival, but in reverse, and usually before dawn. At least it was a relatively safe way of covering distance. There was only one derailment – thankfully, nothing was overturned – but that incident rather delayed the arrival of the tanks, and completely paralysed that section of the *Bundesbahn* network for days on end.

When, for whatever reason, the train was not an option, the limited tank transporter fleet of the British Army would be employed. For most of Chieftain's lifetime, this was the 'Mighty Antar', an impressive, though ancient vehicle and horribly uncomfortable to travel in. Rumour had it that the seats were designed that way, to keep you awake. Towards the end of the Cold War, it was replaced by the Scammel commander, an excellent vehicle. Intelligently, (and as this book has already demonstrated, that was vanishingly rare in MOD Procurement) the Scammel had the same engine as the new Challenger 1, so reducing cost, and easing the logistics footprint. The driver had to travel with the tank, while the rest of the crew would follow in the relative comfort of a bus, or huddled in the back of a freezing Bedford Four-Tonner.

Loading a Chieftain onto a tank transporter, especially the Antar trailer, which had an excessive ramp incline, was one of the most terrifying things a driver had to do. It really didn't matter if you had

---

1   *Yellow Handbag* is the nickname of the yellow 24 bottle cardboard case of Herforder Pils, beloved of Squaddies. Much better than that Tennants stuff…

just arrived the week before, or had been doing it for years, it never got easier. You just had to get on with it. The transporter driver, sometimes RCT, but usually Polish contract drivers nicknamed *MoJos* (I never understood why contractors were used), would stand on top of the spare wheel mounted behind the cab, guiding tanks onto the ramps. At this point, the driver would be sweating from head to toe, clenching his bum cheeks as tightly as possible, as the nose of the tank began to point skywards, until sky was all they could see. Whereupon the forward momentum and weight reached tipping point, as 31 of the 62 tons rapidly pivoted downwards onto the trailer. The driver rapidly gripped the hatch opening

Tipping point. (D J Mason)

for dear life, after releasing the sticks (tillers) – but with his foot on the brake, to stop the tank flying forward. Failure to brace themselves could result in a broken nose or worse, as the tank pitched down.

Achieving the correct speed was essential to loading the tank. Too fast, and it would crash down and even ride up the cab, or fall off the side. In severe cases, crashing down, it could burst all the tyres on the trailer, and when that happened, you really would not want to be the driver. In contrast, among the few truly skilled and gifted, extra points for style would be awarded to a driver achieving precise momentum, finely balanced, seesawing his tank back and forth on the middle suspension units, before gently nudging themselves over onto the trailer. Almost all transporter loadings went well, but it was just as nervewracking every time for the driver (not that they would ever admit it) and of course, when you arrived at your destination, it had to be done again, in reverse.

During tank road moves, German road regulations mandated the fitting of "Blinky", a flashing orange light on the turret top, and reflective dazzle panels fixed on the rear of each tank. This didn't seem to help that much, as German motorists still managed to crash with monotonous regularity into the huge, noisy, smoky 62 ton behemoths, even with reflectors, headlights, tail-lights and Blinky all on. They would invariably exclaim "*I didn't see you!*" or "*Where did you come from?*", so proving beyond all doubt the effectiveness of the standard Green and Black camo. Strangely, nobody ever hit a Berlin Brigade camouflaged tank.

The Antar's superb replacement – the Scammel Commander. (Alan Brown)

Big boy's train set! 11 in view, of 14 (a Squadron) on the train. 62 short tons each = 868 tons. Then the crew carriage, and the rolling stock. And just the one loco. (H Robinson)

Loading onto flatcars – not chained down yet. (Steve Terry)

I never touched the sticks! Honest! (Michael Handley)

Oh, blinking flip! 4 RTR having a bad day. The train having departed. (John Dixon)

Well, there goes the loading schedule! Outside Swinton Barracks, Münster. (Michael Handley)

Another one bites the dust. (Paul Husband)

Gentle sideswipe from Chief-tain = destroyed car and not even scratched paint on the tank. (Derek Dobson)

A Stalwart UBRE in action, refuelling two tanks at once. D Sqn, 1 RTR, Soltau, 1989. (RK)

A field replenishment on Soltau Ranges. (RK)

As mentioned previously, the Infra-Red equipment was not popular, and became used less the longer Chieftain was in service. About the only practical use for the searchlight was to blind the suicidal and arrogant West German HGV drivers, who loved to play chicken with tanks, or any other traffic, at night, with wild overtaking manoeuvres, driving down the crown of the road. After being hit by the full force of the white light searchlight a few times, they soon altered their behaviour.

Reckless motorists would try and overtake tank convoys, attempting to slot themselves in the gaps between tanks, as oncoming vehicles approached. But often during a road move, there wasn't sufficient space left between the slow moving tanks, and very severe damage would result – but only to the car.

In a particularly memorable incident, a brand new BMW shot out of a Army Camp main gate, the oncoming Chieftain swerved, but sideswiped the car causing significant damage. The enraged car driver – an RMP Sergeant Major – climbed out and began screaming at the tank driver and crew, berating and blaming them. He then very unwisely exclaimed "*Couldn't you do any more damage?!?*" Unfortunately for him, the driver was even more crazy than most, and replied "*Yes, I can!*" promptly reversing over the wrecked car, to the utter disbelief of the RMP Sergeant Major.

The fuel tanks of a Chieftain can hold 390 gallons. It had the most appalling fuel economy, of around a gallon a mile, or less over rough terrain. In view of that, many readers may be surprised to learn that refuelling in the field was originally done by manhandling five-gallon jerrycans, just as it had been in the Second World War, so imposing huge demands on the already overworked crews. By all accounts, it was backbreaking work, almost certainly the worst job the early crews ever had. How this was ever considered acceptable in a war fighting situation is beyond comprehension. This complete idiocy was finally done away with in the early '80s, when concerns about the improved air attack and night fighting capability of the Warsaw Pact could no longer be ignored, and it was no longer considered safe to resupply "at leisure" under the cover of darkness. The solution was UBRE, Unit Bulk Refuelling Equipment. This was basically a generator running high pressure fuel pumps, fed by large capacity tanks. UBREs could be mounted on pretty much any moving flat surface, but were commonly fitted to a Stalwart or Bedford Four Tonner. Refuelling was accomplished in just a few minutes. Simple and effective.

With the introduction of the true night fighting capability of TOGS, (and the erroneous assumption that the Russians had something similar) concerns about improved Warsaw Pact capabilities multiplied, and so BAOR's tactical doctrine was given a radical overhaul. In the case of Armoured Operations, the resupply of tanks in the field was to now be accomplished in the style of an extended Formula 1 pit stop (albeit in slow motion!), where fuel, ammunition and food were taken on at a series of short stops, preferably under cover, and with the engine running at all times. (L60 permitting…)

At least one crewman would be scanning the sky, looking for enemy aircraft, and if spotted, the tanks would scatter (rather slowly) for cover. The resupply was usually conducted on a troop by troop basis, so a whole tank Squadron could not be destroyed if caught by the enemy. Troop leaders would be advised by encrypted radio message of the resupply rendezvous point grid reference and required time. Here, they would take on fuel from the UBREs (one tank each side, engine running – "hot refuelling" – then proceed a few hundred yards to an ammo truck, where the loader would call for whichever types of rounds were needed. These would be rapidly dumped onto the turret basket, for sorting out inside the tank later. A bit further down the road, if all was well, there would be the SQMS crew, heaving four-man compo ration packs onto the tanks, exchanging empty water jerry cans for full ones (*no exchange, no water!*) and, if you were lucky, freshly cooked egg banjos and bacon butties, and possibly some mail. But if you were really unlucky, a slop jockey (ACC – Army Catering Corps /Aldershot Concrete Company) cook would dispense a glutinous dollop of the infamous "range stew" and two slices of bread into your mess tins. After grabbing this, the always grateful crew would move on quickly, seeking shelter from imaginary or real marauding *Hind* helicopters, and the next tank troop would emerge from hiding to make its own rapid resupply run.

I was parked. He never saw us. (Alan Robertson)

The Battle Run

The British Army trained to fight the Russians, planning a staged retreat through the German plains, using long range sniping, deliberately falling back as the Russians neared the (shorter) effective range of their own main guns. The intent was to destroy them before they could fight, demoralising them while eroding their numerical superiority. Sadly, most other NATO nations, if not all, still trained with the quaint idea of vast, sweeping, triumphal advances towards the enemy, while firing on the move, evoking the style, *élan*, panache, flair and utter futility of the 1854 Charge of the Light Brigade. Multinational gunnery competitions were unfortunately predicated on this completely unrealistic style of fighting.

Waiting to start a battle run. (D J Mason)

This is a brief description of a single Chieftain engagement in a Battle Run, which would usually entail firing numerous main gun rounds, both APFSDS and HESH, as well as the co-ax and commander's machine guns.

In Germany, the main gun rounds would be special training rounds with a weaker bag charge, as the ranges there were not long enough for full power ammunition to be used.

The engine is screaming at high revs, as the tank lurches and bounces over rough ground. The commands and responses are made over the intercom.

Commander: FIN! TANK! ON! (I've seen a target, it's a tank, load APFSDS, 'On' meaning I'm looking at the target.)

The driver will slam the brakes on at the first word from the commander, be it FIN, HESH etc., and the tank will come to a stop very, very quickly. This is called the "short halt" and is the preferred way to engage a target in the British Army. The turret begins to swing to lay on to the target.

Loader: LOADED! The Loader will have begun loading the gun, upon hearing the word "Fin" with APFSDS, pulling his safety shield across and flicking the turret safety switch to live, so the gun can fire and he can be stood with another Fin round, ready to reload. All within the space of a few seconds.

Gunner: LAZING! The gunner has acquired the target in his sight, and is now using the laser rangefinder to get accurate range information, which is then displayed in his sight. He then presses the autolay button to ensure the gun is aimed (driven, in technical terms) to the correct firing position. All this is done in the time it takes to speak the word.

Commander: FIRE!!

Gunner: FIRING NOW! The gunner pulls the trigger on the 'N' of Now. There is a Bloody Big Bang (deafness-inducing 98-136 dB) and the massive breech flies backwards at great speed, then slowly returns to its start position, automatically opening for reloading as it does so. The loader will be poised ready with the next round, if required.

Gunner: TARGET! The target has been hit. (Or as my gunner mate would put it – "We hit the F*%!£r – we *never* miss!")

Commander: TARGET STOP! The commander confirms the hit and ends the engagement. If the unthinkable has happened, and the gunner *has* missed, (and God help him if he has!) the commander will issue corrections. Otherwise, he will be searching for a new target.

The driver accelerates away on the 'T' of Target Stop.

All of the above actions will have taken place in less time than it took you to read this – from start to finish, ten to fourteen seconds. Dry text sadly cannot convey the noise, smells and rush of adrenaline which comes with taking part in a battle run, but I hope this gives you some idea what it's like.

RK / Karl Lloyd

The instant of firing caught on camera.
1 RTR, Hohne Ranges 1991. (N. Palmer)

Chapter Nine

BATUS

The British Army Training Unit Suffield (BATUS), near Medicine Hat, Alberta, Canada, was first established in 1972. The extensive training area owes its existence to the increasingly difficult and un-realistic training conditions the West German government was imposing. The earlier loss of extensive training grounds in Libya, following Colonel Gadaffi's takeover in 1969, was an additional factor. The British Army began to search for a site able to provide unrestricted training with live ammunition, which was not possible in either the UK or Germany, and found it on the Canadian prairie. The range is big enough to fit every other British Army training space within its boundaries, covering a massive unpop-ulated expanse one tenth the size of Wales, with only one tree in the entire area. (Which is protected by dire threats of death, and even worse, should it be damaged in any way.)

BATUS has had a permanent tank, AFV and wheeled vehicle fleet of over one thousand vehicles, run by a large and well-equipped permanent staff, which now has an OPFOR (opposing force) detachment in residence to provide a realistic enemy. However, that is a new innovation, and was not part of the BATUS setup during the Cold War era. From the 1970s to 1990s, seven three-week exercises known as *Med Man* 1 through 7 were conducted each year.

Med Man referred to Medicine Hat, the nearest large town. (Home to the infamous Assiniboia Inn or 'Sin Bin', as it will forever be known to the many thousands of British soldiers who sampled its charms, wiping their feet on their way out!) Travelling to Canada was a cherished experience for many thousands of squaddies over the years, due to the generous leave allowance provided at the end of each exercise – the opportunity for the aforementioned cultural enrichment, and extended travel with one's companions was always seized. As a result, there are thousands, if not millions, of stories about BATUS and Canada in general told by ex-squaddies – a couple of which are included here, along with a selection of the very photogenic BATUS vehicles and colour schemes.

Range Safety Ferret, 1975
(RK Collection)

If at First, You Don't Succeed – *Blow It Up!*

BATUS was a great place to be in the summer, but not so much in the winter, when the weather gave the North Pole a run for its money. The last exercise of the year, *Med Man 7*, around October, usually had foul weather with deep snow and seriously sub-zero temperatures, which would have made small brass ornamental monkey statues very unhappy. Near the end of one of these Arctic exercises, a Chieftain broke through a thin crust of ice and bogged in. A half-hearted attempt was made to recover it, but with EndEx rapidly approaching, it was abandoned on the area for the permanent staff to recover.

Scrapheap Challenge. (David Bennie)

The REME permanent staff didn't want to leave their nice warm garages in camp, and two weeks passed before they ran out of excuses. They then braved the elements, venturing out to collect the errant tank, which had by this time sunk into the tundra up to the hull and become frozen solid. The ARRV proved incapable of moving the entombed tank, so a second was called out to assist, but even the combined power of two ARRVs, and a Foden recovery truck could not loosen the Chieftain from the clutches of the frozen prairie.

Other possible methods to free the tank were discussed, including pouring fuel round the vehicle and setting fire to it, to melt the ice, which was wisely vetoed. Instead, the Artificer in charge was somehow convinced that detcord (detonation cord), a thin white coloured pipe filled with explosive, laid around the tank, would fracture the ice without damaging the tank. Now, all squaddies *love* blowing things up, and the Royal Engineers love it more than

The moment of truth. (David Bennie)

most, so they gleefully set about wrapping what seemed like the entire world's supply of detcord around the unfortunate tank. After retreating to a safe distance, the explosive was triggered – to devastating effect.

Apparently, the tremor was felt back in Medicine Hat, many, many kilometres away (although that does sound like a slight exaggeration). The detcord did shatter the ice, as promised. Unfortunately, it also pretty much shattered the tank as well, destroying the suspension, ripping the engine from its mountings, destroying the sights, and breaking the tracks. In fact, anything not made of armour plate was annihilated. The recovery crew and RE demolition team thought this was great fun – until they returned to base with the sad remains of the Chieftain on a tank transporter, whereupon the faecal matter hit the rotating air mover at great velocity!

Enquiries were made, charges laid and punishments rapidly dispensed. What remained of the Chieftain was shipped back to the UK for capital rebuild, or scrapping, depending on who you ask. Meanwhile, the Powers That Be tried, and failed, to cover up what had happened. The accompanying photos were taken by one of the REME recovery team, and he has kindly allowed them to be printed here for the first time.

The BATUS training area is a vast, almost featureless plain, with some gentle undulations, and the occasional rare natural landmark. While it was long accepted that Officers could not read maps, unfortunately, nor could some of the rank and file. So aids to navigation such as the 'Coke Bottle Tower' were created.

1 RTR on the prairie in a BATUS Fleet Mk 9. (H Robinson)

On one Medman, the aforementioned *'Flask'* got his tank hopelessly lost, and the Sqn OC became increasingly exasperated, enquiring over the radio as to his whereabouts, in the usual succinct Army style.

"Sgt xxxxxx, where the f*** are you?"

To which *The Flask* replied: *"Canada, Sir!"*

Given the severe weather conditions encountered on Med Man 7, and the live firing by all – tanks, Infantry and worst of all, the Royal Artillery (who weren't nicknamed *"Dropshorts"* for nothing!) – getting lost on the Prairies was no laughing matter, and sadly, fatalities did happen. Over 45 years of training, there have been 42 deaths, mainly (at least officially) as a result of road accidents.

BATUS and OPFOR camouflage

When the Army began operating in Canada, it was obvious the standard NATO scheme of Green and Black stood out on the prairies like a sore thumb. As the idea was to give Battle Groups as realistic a training regime as possible, a new scheme was quickly developed by substituting the NATO Black with the standard British desert colour of Mid-Stone. This scheme was later adopted for the OPFOR (Opposing Forces) Units on Salisbury Plain for training in the UK. OPFOR tanks also usually had their side skirts (bazooka plates) removed for ease of identification.

BATUS vehicles were permanently attached to the base, and each had its own fleet number, the last three numbers of which were painted in white on in a black rectangle on the front bazooka plates. These were nicknamed "BORT" numbers, after the Russian vehicle identification system. Call signs changed from exercise to exercise. As each visiting unit was issued tanks on an ad-hoc basis, the call signs were painted on the turret sides, rear right bin, and occasionally on the bazooka plates.

The turret had two thin white lines painted at 45 degree angles (nicknamed the *forty-fives*), starting between the commander's and loader's hatches, and out over the front of the turret. If there were no vehicles or personnel in between these lines, the tank was allowed to fire live ammunition at targets from its main or auxiliary weapons. In the early 1990s, a vertical white line was painted three quarters down the side of the tank – this was a visual stop line for infantry or other personnel, as being any further forwards risked injury from the firing of the main gun.

BATUS range safety and permanent staff vehicles used the same camouflage scheme, but with a bright post office red top or truck cab. These vehicles were imaginatively named *Redtops*. They also had large call signs painted on the sides and top of the vehicle.

"Ooops..."

Some permanent staff at BATUS became quite blasé about live firing during the exercises, and an unfortunate sense of routine had set in. One of the duties of the Range Safety Staff was to approve the engagement of the hard targets that littered the prairie. Most of these vehicles had long since been turned into piles of unrecognisable scrap, but some were in relatively good condition. The Attacking Forces would ask for permission to engage, giving a grid reference, which was supposed to be checked by the Range Safety Officer.

Oops...

Most of the Officers did check before giving permission to fire – but some did not. One Captain in particular was far too interested in topping up his tan to bother checking, and would lay recumbent on the roof of the Safety Vehicle with his radio, and simply approve all requests, after pausing for the few requisite seconds.

On one very memorable occasion, a FV 432 troop carrier had broken down in the live fire area, and could not be recovered in time before the live firing was due to start. Range Safety were informed of the (vacated) vehicle, and its location. Mere moments after the firing began, an eager tank crew requested permission to engage a target at that grid reference. A few seconds later, the Officer uttered the fateful word "*Granted...*" over the radio. A few more seconds later, a large and impressive explosion reverberated around the area, with a fireball then rising, as the fully loaded and fuelled FV 432 deconstructed itself. After a significant pause, when all radio chatter ceased in astonishment, the offending Officer picked up his radio and simply exclaimed "*Ooops...*"

Destroyed FV 433 (SPG version of the 432). Not enough of the 432 left to photograph! (Duncan Mansfield)

Busy scene – Engine change on the prairie with an ARRV Mk 7 (CHARRV) and dead Chieftain. Meanwhile, dinner is being prepped on the lowered bazooka plate. (Chris Morton)

AVRE carrying fascine (R Ridley, via Wikimedia Commons)

Immaculate Mk 9. Unusually, fitted with SIMFICS. Call sign is for Sqn Commander. (Neil Allen)

Chieftain Mk 5 on the prairie in BATUS. This vehicle has been fitted with the unpopular dozer blade. (RK)

Now tell me again why Chieftains don't need heaters? (RK Collection)

Repairs in the field. The foreground tank has new tracks fitted. 1 RTR, 1988. (H Robinson)

Lost Sqn 2IC explaining how he got into a live firingarea to a disgusted Range Saftey ferret commander. (RK Collection)

3 Troop, 4 RTR, on the last exercise to use Chieftain, 1992. (RK Collection)

Queens Own Hussars battle group drawn up in parade formation Med Man 3 1988. (Jason Kellner)

The BATUS fleet between exercises, early 1989. (RK Collection)

Chapter Ten
Foreign Sales

Due to its high unit cost, and maintenance-intensive nature plus its reputation for unreliability, the Chieftain could not match the outstanding sales success of the Centurion. Furthermore, a prospective customer could buy three used Centurions – with spares – for the price of one Chieftain. None of our NATO allies could be convinced to buy Chieftain, most preferring the overrated, under-armoured, under-gunned but more reliable and much, much cheaper Leopard 1. Nevertheless, significant numbers of Chieftains were sold to various Middle Eastern countries, and it would be wrong to consider it an export failure, as has been claimed. The overseas sales of Chieftain could have been considerably higher but for politics and the intransigent nature of the Government demanding unrealistic prices for the tank. Many countries were very interested in purchasing Chieftain, but were rebuffed, and most of the select few who were allowed to place contracts found that the deal could later be rescinded without warning.

Israel and the Chieftain

In 1964, the Israeli government made the decision that they needed a steady and reliable supply of tanks. The only way to ensure this was to buy a foreign tank, but build it in Israel until the nation could develop its own indigenous armoured vehicles. Initially, the French AMX 30 was considered, as France had been the most sympathetic and reliable supplier of weapons to Israel, and it was considered likely that they would agree to the AMX 30 being built under licence. However, the Israeli Army had begun its love affair with the Centurion, and under the leadership of General Israel Tal had adopted the British "*Big gun heavy armour*" doctrine, and wanted a tank that would better suit this philosophy, rather than one that even the French have admitted was the worst of the first generation MBTs. So, in November 1966, a delegation arrived from the IDF (Israeli Defence Forces) to negotiate an agreement to purchase and subsequently produce the Chieftain under licence in Israel. These negotiations proved difficult and protracted, as the Foreign Office was unhappy with the proposal, as it could offend the Arab countries, which it considered more important, but ultimately, a Memorandum of Understanding was signed, which agreed to establishing a production line in Israel, providing knock-down kits of partially completed Chieftains for final assembly, until the new factory was able to begin production in its own right. In return, Israel committed to sharing its experience in desert warfare, and – most importantly to the Treasury – contributing towards the development costs of the Chieftain (figures vary, but up to 10% of the development costs of Chieftain were paid for by Israel). As part of the agreement, four Chieftain Mk 2s were sent to Israel, the first two for automotive tests, the second pair for gunnery trials.

As the automotive trials in the Negev desert were underway, the outbreak of the Six Day War in June 1967 sent the UK Foreign Office into a panic, and they bombarded the Israelis with increasingly strident demands that the Chieftains be moved away from the border region. The Israeli deadpan reassurance, "*Do not worry, we have moved the Borders*" has to go into the top ten diplomatic responses in history! Rumours followed that the two Chieftains had been involved in the Six Day War, and had returned with their barrels worn smooth from firing, and with shell strikes on the armour. This speculation still circulated on tank parks in the 1990s, and perhaps even today. Even if untrue, an entertaining story.

Overall, the Israelis were impressed with the Chieftain and its performance in desert conditions, especially with the range of the 120 mm gun and its armour, but they had concerns about the lack of power and reliability of the engine. It seems likely that had production gone ahead, the L60 would have been replaced with a reliable diesel engine in very short order.

Conversely, the British also learned a great deal from the trials, the Israeli observations being fed back to ROF Leeds and Vickers-Armstrong in Newcastle. Modifications, such as angling all the sights and

Israeli Mk 4 in Yuma, Arizona. Painted British Mid-Stone. (R Griffin)

commander's episcopes to reduce reflections from the sun, redesigned engine louvres to both aid cooling and prevent shrapnel entering the engine compartment, and installation of a set of IR (Infra-Red) driving lights instead of relying on the main searchlight, all arose from the Israeli trials. Alongside these modifications, the Mk 4 Chieftain was under development to meet the specific requirements of the IDF.

In October 1968, while the trials continued, the Israeli government made an official request to purchase and manufacture the Chieftain under licence. Unfortunately, the political climate in Britain had changed, resulting in a dispute between the Ministry of Defence who approved the proposal, and the Foreign Office who opposed it, with the Cabinet undecided. Unaware of the infighting, the IDF sent another delegation to Britain to study production methods. By December 1969, the Foreign Office view had prevailed, and the British government stunned the Israelis by officially refusing them permission to purchase Chieftain, due to wider political considerations (Israel has no oil). With Britain's refusal to sell them the Chieftain, Israel concluded it could never trust a foreign government to supply its armament needs. General Tal in particular was incensed at what he saw as deliberate betrayal by the British, and consequently began the development of the Merkava tank. The British rejection also followed the refusal of the French Government to supply Mirage Vs to Israel, ultimately leading to the indigenous *Nesher/Kfir* programme. It is clear these refusals to supply advanced weaponry accelerated the establishment of the modern Israeli defence industry. The blocking of sales of Chieftains to Israel was also a shock to the Royal Ordnance Factory and Vickers-Armstrong, which had by this time, built two Mk 4s to Israeli specifications.

These two vehicles were visually quite different to a standard Chieftain, with the rear hull sides built up vertically to increase fuel capacity, the middle suspension unit moved backwards to balance the additional weight of fuel, leaving a large gap between the second and third road wheels, and a return to the original metal tracks, very similar to those fitted to the Centurion (but not the same – Chieftain requires wider and deeper tracks than the Centurion to carry the increased weight). These were better at traversing sand and lighter than the standard rubber-padded tracks. The Mk 4 included many other modifications and improvements, including those previously mentioned, such as the angled episcopes, but the built-up sides, altered road wheel spacing and steel tracks are the most obvious.

With the collapse of the Israeli contract, the two Mk 4s were sent to Yuma, Arizona, for hot desert trials, where they apparently performed well. One was subsequently destroyed in mine damage tests, and the other was returned to the UK. The unique steel tracks were replaced with the standard issue, and the turret removed and replaced with a Coles crane. This hybrid vehicle was used at Kirkcudbright ranges. Its ultimate fate is unknown and subject to rumour, the latest being that it met with an accident, then became a range target.

Perhaps the most shameful part of this whole episode is the speed with which the British Government then offered the Chieftain to Arab nations – after incorporating all the lessons learned from the Israelis. Whatever one's opinion of Israel and its policies, there is no doubt they were treated shamefully.

Libya

Prior to Colonel Gaddafi's coup in September 1969, Britain maintained very good relations with Libya, providing extensive training and equipment for the modernisation of the Libyan armed forces. Col. Gaddafi had in fact seen the Chieftain in operation while attending a training course at Bovington (Army Air Corps Signal Instructors course) prior to his rise to power.

In early 1969, an order for Chieftain MBTs and associated variants (ARV, AVLB) was placed, at a total cost of £25.5 million, of which £9.5 million was paid in advance. The contract covered between 170-188 units (sources vary on the exact number – the majority state 170). Deliveries were scheduled to begin in November 1970, concluding in 1973. The Libyan tanks were designated Mk 3/S (for Sandman). On reflection, quite an insulting name, but typical of the colonial mentality still prevalent in the MOD and Government of the time.

After the revolution, Libya was still keen to take ownership of its Chieftains, but the British Government was unwilling to supply them. Negotiations continued until March 1972, when the British Government finally rescinded the contract, but of course not returning the £9.5 million already paid by Libya. The British Army absorbed the forty (free) Mk 3/S tanks that had already been completed.

Iran

Iran was the major export customer for the Chieftain. In the late 1960s and early 1970s, it was busy buying itself a modern military with its oil and gas revenues. As the Shah was a known Anglophile, it was a predictable and most welcome development when the Imperial Iranian Army approached the British arms industry with an open chequebook. Ironically, the Israelis enjoyed good relations with the Iranians during this period, and General Tal had recommended they buy Chieftain!

In 1971, the Imperial Iranian Army placed an order for 707 Chieftain MBTs, made up of a mixture of Mk 3/3(P) and Mk 5(P), to the same basic specification as the British Army Chieftain, but with a 750

Glory days of the Imperial Iranian Army Chieftains. (RK Collection)

Iranian Chieftains in an Iraqi captured equipment dump. (RK Collection)

Iranian Chieftain. Wouldn't want to be the Driver with that bow wave flooding his compartment. (RK Collection)

hp "export" version of the L60 engine. The Iranian Chieftains retained the ranging gun even if the laser sight and MRS were fitted, which in many cases it appears they were not. The first few hundred Iranian Chieftains had the early version of the 120 mm L11 gun, but the remainder were fitted with the updated L11 A5. Iranian Chieftains also lacked the Improved Fire Control System (IFCS), although this was intended to be retrofitted.

The Iranians also ordered 71 Chieftain Armoured Recovery Vehicles, to an improved specification, including an Atlas crane for engine changes, and the ability to carry a spare L60 pack on the rear deck. As previously outlined, the British Army subsequently upgraded its own Chieftain ARVs to this standard, renaming them Chieftain Armoured Repair and Recovery Vehicles (ARRV). The Iranian order was completed by fourteen Armoured Vehicle Launching Bridges (AVLB) for a grand total of 792 vehicles, plus spares.

However, the Iranian Army did not take to the Chieftain, preferring the much simpler M47/M60 family, which were also more reliable, though they did appreciate the power and range of Chieftain's 120 mm main gun and its heavy armour. While Iran was an industrialised and advanced nation, the Chieftain's complexity and unreliable engine stretched them to their limits and beyond. Eventually, Iran demanded something be done to improve the situation. They wanted an automatic gearbox (easier to use, requiring less driver training to operate), a reliable diesel engine with better fuel consumption, better suspension, improved mine protection and greater fuel capacity. British industry knew that to meet all these requirements meant a new tank which would take years to develop, so an offer was made of an upgraded Chieftain to bridge the gap, until the new tank was ready. This became known as the FV 4030 programme, described earlier in this book. As this book was going to print in an ironic twist to the Iranian Chieftain Story a video appeared on the internet showing Iranian Chieftains being refurbished and fitted with Russian T72 engines for continued service, although the tank shown leaving the rebuild facility was still making the distinctive L60 scream as it pulled away so perhaps it was all propaganda?

Kuwait

In 1976, Kuwait placed an order for 175 (some sources say 176-9) Chieftain Mk 5/2K (for Kuwait). These Chieftains were identical to the latest British Army specification, and included the TLS, MRS and IFCS. Externally, the only way to differentiate a Chieftain Mk 5/2 and Mk 5/2K was by the large stowage box placed inside the loader's basket on the Mk 5/2K. The Kuwaitis, in contrast to the Iranians, loved their Chieftains, and kept them in service until the early 1990s, when they began to be replaced with Yugoslav M84s. At least thirty were still kept in war storage at the turn of the millennium. Sadly, the remaining Kuwaiti Chieftains are now in open storage in the desert, some still fully loaded with ammunition and Complete Equipment Schedule. Others have been used as targets for air delivered weaponry.

Kuwaiti Mk 5(K) prior to delivery doing doughnuts at Barnbow. (ROF Leeds). (RK Collection)

Oman

The Sultan of Oman's Armed Forces received a single Squadron (twelve) of Chieftain Mk 7/2 C tanks, leased in 1981. These were refurbished tanks from British Army stocks, later purchased by Oman, alongside an order for fifteen new-build vehicles, which the ROF Leeds unofficially named the Mk 15, while the Omanis titled them *Qayd Al Ardh*. The new-build Chieftains were built to Mk 5/3 standard. All fifteen were delivered by 1985, and with that delivery, the Chieftain production line finally closed. These Chieftains have also now left Omani service. Two serve as Gate Guards, and one is in a museum. The rest await an uncertain fate.

Oman was also given an ARRV by Jordan, as the price for a new-build was quoted as £1 million. The favour was later repaid, as when Oman replaced their Chieftains (with the Challenger 2) all usable spares were gifted to Jordan and the ARRV returned.

Iraq

Iraq captured a large number of Chieftains during the Iran-Iraq War. No accurate number is known, but it is believed to be at least one hundred, and possibly as high as 190. Many were simply abandoned in full working order by their Iranian crews. A group of Iranian dissidents known as the *Mujaheddin-e – Khaliq* (National Liberation Army), who had helped overthrow the Shah but then fell foul of the new regime, was formed into a fighting unit around 1982, and issued thirty or more captured Chieftains. Initially, the crews were not entirely trusted, being issued with limited fuel and ammunition loads. But they did see action, and soon gained the full trust of the Iraqis. While there is no confirmed proof, there is a strong possibility that Chieftain has faced Chieftain in battle.

The remainder of the captured tanks were stripped for spares, and some were later donated to Jordan. The Iraqis also purchased fifty Chieftain ARVs, originally intended for Iran, in a questionable deal where Jordan was used as a middle-man, to avoid the sanctions placed on Iraq.

Serious negotiations took place in the 1980s between the British Government and Iraq to allow the latter to purchase the Chieftain or the *Shir* 2, but these came to nothing, due to the high price demanded by the British Government, and its fear of the Russians gaining access to the Chobham armour of the *Shir* 2. The Iraqis later absorbed the captured Chieftains of the Kuwaiti Army and integrated them into its armoured forces. It later returned over sixty to Kuwait, after the end of the First Gulf War.

An Iraqi Mk 7 ARRV towing a T-55 retreating from Kuwait, which has succumbed to an engine fire. (RK Collection)

Iraqi boneyard following 2nd Gulf War. (RK Collection)

Mujaheddin – e-Khaliq crest.

Iraqi Chieftain refurbished at Basra in 2015. Note the non-standard side skirt bazooka plates. (RK Collection)

A graveyard of Iraqi armour, including Chieftains, was established at Taji, ten miles north of Baghdad, after the Second Gulf War in 2003. Pictures of the graffiti-covered vehicles there are well known on the internet. Recently, photos appeared of some Chieftains being refurbished for supposed service with the Iraqis in Basra in 2015, while other sources claim they were in fact sold back to the Iranians, to reinforce their dwindling fleet. As this book was being prepared for publication, in late 2017, more photographs appeared via Twitter, showing several Chieftain Mk 5s after refurbishment at the heavy engineering facility of the Ibn Majid State Company in Basra. Perhaps these are being returned to service with the Iraqis, but it seems far more likely that they are destined to rejoin their original owners.

Iraqi Chieftain at the boneyard. (RK Collection)

Jordan

After the Iranian Revolution in 1979, and the cancellation of all Iranian orders, the British government found itself with a huge problem. The Shah of Iran had been almost single-handedly keeping the British arms industry afloat, and they were now faced with the possible closure of ROF Leeds and Vickers in Newcastle, with massive job losses, which could not be allowed to happen.

Frantic sales drives and diplomatic talks resulted in a Jordanian order for 274 FV 4030/1 *Shir* 1 (which had been hastily renamed the *Khalid*), and with some modifications to suit the Jordanian Army, and at a knock-down price of £276M, the ROF and Vickers were saved from closure. While they were not pure Chieftains – they were a developed version rather than a new tank – they are listed here. The *Khalid* still serves alongside the Challenger 1 fleet later acquired by the Jordanians. So it could be claimed that the Jordanians still have both the *Shir* 1 and *Shir* 2 in service.

Jordanian Fake Khalid – Chieftain at the Military Technical Museum in Lešany, Czech Republic, 2010. Described incorrectly as a Khalid on Wikipedia. (Adamicz, via Wikimedia Commons)

As previously mentioned, Jordan was given a number of Chieftains by Iraq as a gift for assistance rendered during the Iran-Iraq War. Jordan had little use for them, beyond providing spare road wheels and gun barrels, and they have sat rusting in the desert ever since. One example (misidentified on Wikipedia as a *Khalid*) has been kept in running order at the Lešany Military Technical Museum, located some 20 km south of Prague. This is shown in the '*Preserved Examples*' Annex. This was swapped for another exhibit for inclusion in the brand new Jordanian Royal Tank Museum. Another is now held in that museum's collection, along with a *Khalid*.

Chapter Eleven

The Chieftain in Action

The Iran-Iraq War

Saddam Hussein's Iraq invaded the oil-rich Iranian province of Khuzestan on 22nd September 1980, hoping to take advantage of the chaos in Iran after the 1979 revolution, and settle a long standing territorial dispute. Prior to the revolution, the Imperial Iranian Armed forces had been the fifth largest Army in the world, and one of the best equipped. However, the majority of the ground forces had not been well trained, leading to a situation perhaps best described as "all the gear and no idea" (a British Army insult often aimed at Americans!).

Purges following the revolution had decimated the Iranian Army's Officer Corps and even the NCO ranks of the Army. Much of the cutting-edge equipment had either been destroyed, or was unserviceable due to lack of spares. Astonishingly, most of the regular Army Infantry units had been disbanded. Tank strength had fallen from 1,700 to just over 1,000, a mix of Chieftain, M60, M47 and M48s. Given this situation, it is remarkable – and perhaps a reflection of how poor the Iraqi Army also was – that the Iranians were able to resist the invasion, and eventually push the Iraqis out of Iran. Details of the battles and use of armour are still hard to find, but some information is known.

A well-used Iranian Mk 3 loaded with extra supplies during the Iran-Iraq war. (RK Collection)

First Battle of Khorramshahr

During the opening phase of the war, a huge force of Iraqis advanced on the city of Khorramshahr, supported by five hundred T-55 and T-62 tanks. The city was defended by a scratch force of Iranian regular and paramilitary units, which included one squadron of Chieftains from the 92nd Tank division,

which was, and still is, considered an elite Iranian unit. The Iraqi forces made steady advances, except when they encountered the Chieftains, which repeatedly stopped them dead, inflicting heavy casualties on their armour. They were such a problem that the Iraqis withdrew and set up siege lines. The Chieftains were destroyed in coordinated surprise attacks as part of a wider Special Forces offensive, and Khorramshahr fell soon after.

Battle of Abadan

It had been the intention of the Iraqi forces to seize Abadan in the first days of the war, but Khorramshahr delayed them and absorbed more and more of their forces. While some minor actions took place, it was not until June 1981 that the Iraqis launched a determined attack to take Abadan, despite being outnumbered 4:1. The Iranians repulsed the Iraqi units. The 92nd Armoured Division were deployed in the city with 50–60 tanks, facing up to 400 Iraqi T-55 and T-62s. The Chieftain's strong armour and long range gun again proved very effective, capable of taking out the enemy tanks long before they came into their own maximum range, just as it was supposed to.

In September 1981, the Iranians launched an operation to relieve Abadan and push the Iraqis back. They succeeded, but at great cost. The lack of planning and reckless use of armour to support 'human wave' charges left thousands dead and 170 tanks, including many Chieftains, wrecked on the battlefield.

In October the Iraqis launched a surprise attack on Iranian positions and ambushed a supply column guarded by a large force of Chieftains from the 16th Armoured Division. The Iranians apparently either fled without firing a shot, or simply abandoned their tanks, leaving the bewildered Iraqis in possession of over twenty fully operational Chieftains. This action demonstrates the difference between well trained and led units such as the 92nd Armoured Division, and the mostly conscript and poorly trained 16th Armoured Division.

An Imperial Iranian Army Chieftain joins the Islamic Republic of Iran Army. (RK Collection)

In combat behind a sand berm. Note the infantryman firing – but not aiming. (RTC Collection)

Operation *Nasr*

Operation *Nasr* was conceived as part of a larger plan to push the Iraqis out of Iran and break the siege of Abadan, but became hijacked by politicians and the rivalry between the Regular Army and *Pasdaran* (Iranian Revolutionary Guards Corps). The Army was in no fit state to conduct the operation, which was badly planned due to the lack of competent Staff Officers and Commanders, lacking the required superiority of numbers, on terrain completely unsuited for tanks – deep mud which turned into a quagmire during rain, forcing the tanks to keep to the few paved roads. Reconnaissance was almost non-existent, as was security.

The Iranians committed over 300 tanks from the 16th Armoured Division, the usual mix of Chieftains and M60, M47 and M48s, and large amounts of support equipment to the operation. Due to the lack of operational security, the Iraqis were well aware of the plan. When the Iranians attacked, using three pontoon bridges to cross the Karkheh River, the Iraqis lured them into an almost perfect trap with dug-in tanks on three sides in a box formation. The advancing Iranian armour charged into the trap and was promptly massacred by the emplaced armour. The American tanks suffered more than the Chieftains, due to their thinner armour, and because ammunition was stored in the turret, almost guaranteeing the destruction of the tank from internal explosions if penetrated.

The Iranians tried to force a way through the ambush, but the road became blocked by destroyed and damaged tanks. Attempts were made to leave the road, but the tanks became bogged down in the mud, and the Iranian attack descended into chaos. An order was given to retreat, which led to panic breaking out amongst the poorly trained crews, being sitting ducks on the road. Command and discipline started dissolving like a sandcastle in the rain. All the conditions were in place for a comprehensive rout and decisive victory for the Iraqis when the pontoon bridges over the river were destroyed by artillery fire, cutting off the escape route. In response to this, the Iranians then seemed to become resigned to their fate, and decided to take as many Iraqis with them as possible; the Chieftain crews began engaging the dug-in hull-down Iraqi tanks, inflicting heavy and unexpected casualties on them. Chieftain's 120 mm gun and fire control system proved superior to anything else on the battlefield.

Meanwhile, heroic efforts by Iranian engineers re-established a pontoon bridge across the river, and an orderly withdrawal was then conducted, with the Chieftains acting as rearguard using their heavy armour and resistance to hits and powerful guns to cover the retreating forces. This engagement showed that the Chieftain's frontal arc could withstand anything the T-55 or T-62 could throw at it, and if penetrated through the weaker side armour the two-part ammunition in the protected charge bins did not cook off instantly, if at all, giving the crew a chance to escape.

Operation *Nasr* was the largest tank battle of the Iran-Iraq war, and despite the losses they suffered was an Iraqi victory. Iran had lost between 10-20% of its total remaining tanks and armoured vehicles.

Iranian Chieftain used as dug in strongpoint. (RK Collection)

A devastating blow, as losses could not be replaced – approximately two hundred tanks, plus another hundred AFVs and self propelled guns, were either destroyed or captured. In turn, the Chieftains claimed over one hundred Iraqi tanks and other armoured vehicles, heavy losses for such a well planned and executed ambush.

After this action, the war became one of stalemate and futility, with Iran relying on massed human wave attacks and the Revolutionary Guards, to make up for a lack of equipment. Most of the remaining Chieftains seemed to have been used as static artillery or dug-in strongpoints. A ceasefire was agreed by Iran in August 1988.

Operation *Mersad*

Six days after the ceasefire later, the *Mujahadeen-e-Khalq* (MEK) (National Liberation Army), an Iranian dissident group supported by Saddam Hussein and equipped with at least thirty Chieftains, launched Operation *Forough Javidan* (Eternal Light) on the Central Front. Deploying around 7,000 irregulars, this attack, or "liberation" as the MEK claimed, initially had great success, being supported by heavy Iraqi air cover, penetrating 90 miles (145 km) deep into Iran and meeting only weak resistance. The ultimate objective of the invaders was to reach Tehran and overthrow the Islamic Government. The MEK leadership expected that a popular uprising would take place, unaware of the level of hatred held for what was known as "the traitorous MEK" by ordinary Iranians. Once the incursion reached beyond its effective air cover, the fate of the MEK was sealed. The Iranian High Command had begun moving significant forces to shore up its ravaged defences on the Southern Front, but the IRIA (Islamic Republic of Iran Army) was able to divert the redeployment and prepare an elaborate plan, Operation *Mersad* (ambush), very similar to that which they themselves had been subjected to in Operation *Nasr* early in the war. On 28th July 34 km west of Bakhtaran, the invading forces ran headlong into the trap, being taken under fire from three sides and annihilated. Over 120 tanks, including the Chieftains and many other armoured and soft skin vehicles, were destroyed and large numbers of MEK soldiers killed. The survivors were routed, as the Iranian Army retook the briefly occupied towns leading back to the border. Iranian equipment loss and casualty figures are not known, but would appear to have been very light. As it was IRIA units including the 16th Armd Division which engaged the MEK, there is a strong possibility that Chieftain fought against Chieftain during this final battle of the war.

Postwar, the Iranian forces had an estimated 300 to 350 Chieftains left. Although official sources maintain that no spares were supplied to Iran during the war, others claim parts were supplied. It seems unlikely that a depleted force of even three hundred Chieftains could be kept operational without a steady stream of L60 engines, in addition to the other myriad logistics demanded by a complex weapons system such as the Chieftain.

Once More Unto the Breach – British Chieftains go to War

During Op *Granby*, the Royal Engineers Willich AVREs were the first tanks over the line, from 0400 hrs on 24th February 1991. They breached the Iraqi sand berm defences with dozer blades, and blasted their way through minefields by launching Giant Vipers from towed trailers. AVLBs were also deployed.

While the Special Purpose Vehicles then lagged behind the Challenger MBT spearhead, it was these Chieftains which removed Saddam's obstacles and cleared the way. REME CHARRVs provided further vital but unseen supporting roles in the build-up, and later recovered some of the few intact abandoned Iraqi tanks as trophies of war, some of which can now be seen in UK museums.

32 Armoured Engineer Regiment demonstrating the mine plough equipped AVLB to US Forces, prior to the ground campaign. (Paul Welling)

AVLB with Number 9 bridge, first day of land campaign, 1991. (Paul Welling)

The added weight of the plough and associated equipment acted as an anchor when reversing onto a tank transporter. Note orange ID panel – and state of bridge. (Paul Welling)

Reverse Charge! The driver became impatient and put his foot down – with dramatic effect! Luckily the powerful brakes saved it from taking out the transporter cab. (Paul Welling)

The reversing drama over, the AVLB is nudged into place for the move south to Saudi Arabia. (Paul Welling)

AVLB in theatre, 1991. Note additional side armour from Warrior, and mine plough in use, also towing Giant Viper trailer. (Paul Welling)

CHARRV removes engine from Challenger, 1991. (RK Collection)

Chieftain's finest hour
– The Defence of Kuwait and the
Battle of the Bridges

Iraq launched its invasion of Kuwait at midnight on 1st August 1990. The Kuwaitis were taken completely by surprise. With their armed forces still operating a peacetime routine, an emergency mobilisation began against a background of confusion and wild rumours. The Kuwaiti 35th *Shaheed* (Martyrs) Armoured Brigade was under the Command of Col Salem Masoud Al Sorour, and it responded quickly with all it had available. The 35th had two Armoured Battalions, the 7th and 8th. The 7th Battalion had a large proportion of its troops on leave, or detached to peacetime guard duties in other areas of Kuwait. The Operations Officer began a frantic round of phone calls to recall personnel, as well as confirming with all present at the base whether they had any training on Chieftains. This rapid response generated

27 scratch crews. The 8th Battalion had been sent, without its tanks, to guard oilfields, and the majority of its personnel would play no part in the defence of Kuwait.

The Commander of the 8th had sent its 3rd Company back from the oilfields, and they were now working alongside the 7th Battalion with ten crews, frantically trying to provision the Chieftains with full war loads, and powering up the operating systems and attempting to boresight the main guns to ensure accuracy. (In peacetime, tanks do not carry ammunition, rations or large amounts of fuel on board.) The following eight hours passed in a blur, and inevitably, the Chieftains did not have a full loadout when they departed their barracks. Nor had they been able to complete boresighting, always a long and difficult job, even under the best of circumstances, which these were not. But the most significant omission was a lack of drinking water for the crews, which would cause severe difficulties in the extreme summer heat of Kuwait. The 7th Brigade left first, led by Lt Col Alwazan, whose Chieftain promptly broke down just outside the gates, reducing the 7th to 26 tanks, split into three Companies of ten, nine and seven. They were directed into position hidden in a cemetery north of the 6th Ring Road. This was a large six-lane highway running round the outskirts of Kuwait City, which gave them a commanding position covering the two main roads connecting to the ring road, which the Iraqis had to travel down to enter the city.

At 06.45, almost immediately after the Kuwaitis had taken up position, the lead elements of the Iraqi *Hammurabi* Division turned onto the 6th Ring Road, directly in front of the Chieftain's positions. They were in road column, with no attempt to protect their flanks, as if on parade, presenting a perfect target – which the Kuwaitis took full advantage of, inflicting heavy losses on the Iraqis. Initially, the inexperienced scratch crews of the Chieftains were all firing on the same target, extremely unfortunate for the targeted vehicles, which ceased to exist, but a waste of ammunition. Company Commanders directed the crews to engage individual targets, giving each tank its own sector to cover.

An order from the High Command was received, directing all tanks to cease fire and return to base. The firing stopped for a few minutes and the Iraqis pushed vehicles down the road, still in column. The Brigade Commander got on the radio and according to his report, "*explained the order from HQ was inappropriate, and directed the resumption of firing.*" This is flowery official Arabic language for "*Screamed blue murder and told them to get on with destroying the Iraqis.*" Firing resumed, and many Iraqi tanks and vehicles were destroyed, including a 2S1 *Gvozdika* self-propelled howitzer which exploded, also destroying its transporter – a "*twofer*" in British Army slang.

The Chieftains were engaging the Iraqis at 1,000-1,500 metres (0.6 – 0.9 miles), virtually point blank range, and even with guns which had not been boresighted, it was almost impossible for them to miss. As the 7th was reducing the *Hammurabi* Division's vehicles to scrap, the 3rd Company of 8th Battalion (which had been delayed by an abortive attempt to relieve the Kuwaiti 80th Brigade, trapped in its barracks by the Iraqis) was pulling into position south of the second (Salmi) Road. Here, it could support the 7th, while covering both bridges onto the ring road, and the approach down from the Mutlaa Ridge.

Kuwaiti anti-tank teams from the attached infantry units at first thought they were Iraqis, but the distinctive Chieftain engine noise and smoke stopped them firing. The Commander of the 3rd Company,

Kuwaiti 35th Brigade Chieftain after the first Gulf War. (RK Collection)

Capt Ali Abdulkareem, quickly grasped the situation, and began firing on the Iraqis on the ring road. A column of infantry trucks was engaged. Hundreds of Iraqis poured out of them, only to sit down at the side of the road, and watch the action for the rest of the day, without taking any part in it. Some Iraqis even tried to surrender, but were turned away, as the Kuwaitis did not have the manpower to accept prisoners.

In a somewhat surreal turn of events during the initial engagement, a taxi pulled up alongside the 3rd Company tanks. The best gunner in the 8th Battalion, who had been on leave, emerged, still in his civilian clothes, calmly paid the driver, and then enquired which tank he should go to. The Company Commander grabbed him and soon put him to work.

The Iraqi *Hammurabi* division was stopped dead in its tracks, and withdrew to positions back over the Mutlaa Ridge, playing little further part in the battle. While sporadic artillery exchanges took place, the Chieftains received some ineffectual small arms fire, then there was a lull in the battle. A very enterprising Kuwaiti Arab water seller appeared on the roadside, selling water to both Iraqi and Kuwaiti soldiers (both currencies accepted!) who lined up peacefully next to each other, chatting while waiting. Another surreal moment, not exactly the Christmas truce of 1914, but worthy of mention. During the lull, vehicles were dispatched back to the Brigade base to bring more ammunition, which they succeeded in doing.

At around 11:00am, Kuwaiti reconnaissance spotted another large column approaching down the Salmi Road. Hopes that this was a relief force from the Gulf Co-operation Council were soon dashed, when T-72s were seen in the vanguard. The 7th Brigade redeployed some of its tanks so it could cover the northern side of the road, while still blocking the first bridge and ring road. The advancing force was the Iraqi *Medina* Armoured Division, and amazingly it had not been informed of the Kuwaiti resistance, and came down that road in the same fashion that the *Hammurabi* had – in parade formation, with no reconnaissance or flank guard. One insanely brave Kuwaiti officer walked up to the Iraqis, and asked them to identify themselves, which they did, even going so far as to name their Commander. The officer thanked them, and returned to his unit, where he reported the information, and prepared to engage the Iraqis.

The Kuwaitis allowed the Iraqis to turn onto the ring road, effectively letting them drive through the middle of them, before opening fire from either side and their rear. The Iraqis had no idea where the incoming fire was coming from, and panicked. Two T-72s reversed wildly, careering through the bridge barriers, crashing to the ground some forty feet below. The Kuwaitis continued to destroy anything that moved. One platoon of T-72s, better led than the others, tried to outflank the 3rd Company, but was spotted and wiped out as soon as they broke cover. This proved the last straw for the Iraqis, who broke

The victors of the Battle of the Bridges rotting in the desert today. (P Breakspear)

and drove back the way they had come, while the 35th Brigade's 26 Chieftains calmly picked off stragglers until they reached cover. The Iraqis stopped to regroup at a truck weighing station. Unfortunately for them, the attached (but under strength) Artillery Battalion of the 35th Brigade had been watching them, commanded by the previously mentioned officer. He ordered his men to open fire, dropping high explosive shells with deadly accuracy onto the Iraqis, who took off like scalded cats back over the Mutlaa Ridge. The *Medina* Division showed more fight than the *Hammurabi*, and quickly reorganised and attacked back over the ridge, and down the Salmi Road, where they were again engaged by the tanks of the 35th Brigade.

The Kuwaitis were now running out of ammunition. With most of his tanks down to only two or three main gun rounds, and some even out of ammunition, with no prospect of help or resupply, Col. Salem, the Brigade Commander, was forced to withdraw his Chieftains south of the Salmi Road, to prevent his force being surrounded. Vehicles were again dispatched to the Brigade barracks to get more ammunition, only to find the camp was now in the hands of the Iraqis. Virtually out of ammunition, and running low on other supplies, the 35th withdrew south towards the Saudi border, where they spent the night, only crossing into Saudi Arabia the next morning, when it was clear that Kuwait had fallen. During the battle, they had only lost three Chieftains, one to engine failure and the other two to enemy air strikes while withdrawing over the Saudi Arabian border. Iraqi losses are unclear, but a conservative estimate is over seventy T-72s, and over one hundred other armoured vehicles destroyed, not including trucks and transporters. This battle is the source of the quote *"our Chieftains opened their T-72s like beautiful flowers"*, not the other way round, as often misquoted by apologists for Russian armour.

Chieftain had proved her mettle in battle. When used correctly, it was a devastating weapon. Credible post-battle analysis suggested that if the Kuwaitis had been mobilised, and the 35th been able to deploy in full strength, then it would have been able to halt the Iraqi advance, allowing Gulf Coalition forces to reinforce them, so preventing Kuwait from being occupied, thereby removing the reason for the First Gulf War. As it was, a scratch force had stopped elements of two supposedly elite divisions cold, for over ten hours.

As if that was not good enough, and to show that tanks, especially Chieftains, do not operate in isolation, the day after the Kuwaitis crossed into Saudi Arabia, the Maintenance Officer for the 35th, Captain Nasser Al-Dewailah, returned to Kuwait City with a small team of volunteers. They brazenly repaired tanks which had been abandoned on the city streets the previous day due to mechanical problems, and drove them over the border.

Nor does the story end there. Capt Nasser and his team of clerks and storemen drove back into Kuwait City again, into the 35th Brigade's base on the third and fourth days after the invasion. They loaded the majority of the Brigade's spares onto trucks, which were then driven to the camp in Saudi Arabia, thus allowing the Chieftains to be maintained and serviced, ready to return to Kuwait as part of the Coalition Forces. When asked how he managed to gain access to a military base occupied by the Iraqis, Capt Nasser explained that the occupiers were too busy looting the colour TV sets and other electrical appliances from the barracks to take any notice of anyone helping themselves to tank parts.

When the Multinational Coalition began to deploy to Saudi Arabia, the 35th Brigade was assigned to work with the US Marines and the attached British 7th Armoured Brigade, as the British Challengers had some limited spares commonality. British REME units were detached to help keep the Kuwaiti Chieftains ready for battle. The arrival of the 4th Armoured Brigade, to make up a full British Division, meant that the British forces were removed from their supporting role with the US Marines and the 35th Brigade. The Kuwaitis stayed with the Marines and advanced with them to liberate Kuwait City. When asked how their return to Kuwait went, Col Salem Masoud Al Sorour, Commander of the 35th Brigade replied, *"Much quieter, the Iraqis shelled us once, but American air power silenced them."*

The Chieftain story is perfectly summed up by the following quote from an unknown officer of the Kuwaiti 35th *Shaheed* Brigade, interviewed by the BBC during the preparations to liberate Kuwait.

"Our Chieftains are the best tanks in the world, and we will prove it again in battle – if only we can get them there..."

Chapter Twelve

Walk-rounds and Interiors

Mk 10

The Chieftain Mk 10 saw the first major change to the look of the Chieftain in twenty years, with the addition of the Stillbrew up-armouring on the turret front which restored its frontal invulnerability to any Soviet tank round and ATGW. The vehicle used in this walk-round had a hard life as a corporate team-building toy, before being sold to a private collector. It was used as the reference vehicle for the recent Takom model. The private collection was broken up in 2017. Initially sold to TanksaLot near Northampton, now sadly sold on and shipped to the Middle East where it will be used as a moving range target. A very sad end for yet another Chieftain.

Mk 10 – general view of the subject of this walkround – in a private collection – sadly now sold off.
(All photos RK)

Mk 10 and Willich AVRE together.

Antenna base on top of TUAAM in its external armoured box.

Armoured cover for turret control systems.

Armoured shutter mechanism for Gunner's main sight.

Attachment bracket for smoke dischargers (wiring is missing).

Aux engine exhaust and final drives, which could be disconected to ease towing.

Brackets for spare track links (very rarely used).

Brake disc used to stop tank. Same system as used on modern cars – but very difficult to change.

Commander's storage basket – removed from turret.

Cover for Co-axial machine gun, mounted above main gun.

Cupola wiper motor housing.

Drive sprocket. Note wear pattern – this sprocket has been reversed, probably after it was sold to the private sector.

Drive sprocket.

Driver control panel gear indicator and barrel location repeater. The large white pedal is the brake pedal.

Floor of Driver's compartment, without seat in place, showing storage for two 120 mm HE rounds.

Forward lifting bracket on turret top.

Front view – rubber mudguard has been torn away.

Front view of IR White Light armoured searchlight.

Front view of smoke dischargers (LHS).

GCE Metadyne compartment – a constant source of trouble. The Armoured cover has been removed.

Gun breech, guard and operating levers. The circular lids at bottom left are the refigerated bag charge bin covers.

Gun clamp (late type).

Gunner's emergency sight aperture in Stillbrew package.

Gunner's main sight, and Commander's day – night sight. Bracket to left of cupola was for white light searchlight.

Hatch mechanism. The rubber concertina is supposed to be attached to the underside of the hatch to protect the hydraulic cylinder.

Horstmann suspension unit.

Hot air and water drain on underside of searchlight.

Idler adjustment nut.

Idler wheel – identical for all Mks from the Mk 3 onwards. Note the hex key hole – when undone, the internal oil level could be checked.

Idler wheel.

Loader's basket – note basket within basket to stop contents falling out, and round socket for reel of telephone cable attached to turret.

Loader's position facing forward oval opening is for Co-ax GPMG. Red handled levers control opening of breech and closing of breech guard (in folded position).

Main engine cooling fan. Loose wire is for a temperature sensor.

Main engine fire extingwisher handles in Driver's compartment.

Main Engine starter panel.

Main exhaust pipe – the insert is not standard.

Mantlet cover – note characteristic sag of concertina section.

NBC pack air intake.

Oil scavange tank and LHS brake disc.

Open gearbox compartment. Large silver box is smoke box to reduce exhaust emissions from main engine (didn't work). Exhaust to right is for APU or 'Donkey' engine.

Rear RH mudguard – this is thin sheet metal and bolts to the rear plate for easy replacement.

Rear view under armoured smoke box (exhaust muffler).

Rear view, showing armoured box which (sometimes) contained a phone to allow Infantry to talk to the Commander.

Searchlight basket mounting plate.

Searchlight basket note basket within basket to stop things falling out.

Searchlight rear access plate.

Side view of sloped hull side and clamps for towing cable. The two strange hooks are part of the deep wading kit, never used on Chieftain.

Side view with bazooka plates removed.

Smoke box (exhaust gas expansion and cooling).

Smoke discharger bracket and Stillbrew armour angles.

Stillbrew from turret rear.

Telephone handset on retractable cord.

Towing cable brackets (front).

Towing cable brackets (rear). Cable is turned up as tank has been reversed into hard object and the rear mudguard and bins bent upwards.

Transmission deck, showing main and steering brakes.

TUAM Box with fire extingusher bracket.

Turret casting numbers – usually covered by Commander's bin.

Turret interior Gunner's position. Note recuperators on top of main gun, which is at maximum elevation.

Very very worn road wheel.

Turret – Front view back towards Commander's cupola. Note open cover on Gunner's main sight and slot in Stillbrew for the Tank Laser Sight (TLS).

Turret front showing Stillbrew up-armour package. The bow in the armour is not standard and is a manufacturing defect where the cement has not filled the form.

Turret top – note that the Loader's storage bin is attached to the top of the turret, not the side.

Tracks slotting onto drive sprocket – note tracks are very badly worn they would never be allowed to get into this state on an operational tank.

Mk 11

This immaculate example of a Mk 11 was part of the REME museum reserve collection, which the Author was privileged to gain access to before Bordon closed and the collection was moved onto an (inaccessible) active military base. The Chieftain, however, was sent to Bovington where it is now used as the "reference" Chieftain for any restoration or measurements, due to its condition.

At the time of the walk-round, the TOGS equipment had already been removed for security reasons, but otherwise this vehicle was as "factory fresh" as any Chieftain, having completed its upgrade to Mk 11 spec just prior to its end of service. It was then planned to be destroyed as part of the CFE treaty, but was somehow reprieved.

Chieftain Mk 11.

Additional turret storage bin (same as rear bin) and its mounting.

Antenna base and armoured TUAM box mounted behind Stillbrew frontal armour (note fire extingusher in place below).

Attachment of the splash guard to the headlight brush guards.

Bracket for holding aerials, and extra bin mounting.

Commander's basket – note mesh insert.

Commander's cupola from above.

Commander's basket, with telephone line laying equipment mount.

Commander's cupola periscopes and wipers.

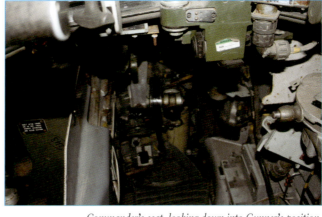

Commander's seat, looking down into Gunner's position.

Commander's seat. Loose cables are where TOGS has been removed. Large black handle is to raise seat.

Concertina and canvas cover at the end of the barrel. Changing this was a hated job for the crews.

Cupola detail of Commander's sight housing (sight missing) and GPMG mount.

Cupola detail with mount for searchlight (left) and GPMG (right).

Dozer blade mount.

Driver's hatch – sight missing – note wading rail is U channel, and Stillbrew armour blocks either side of Driver's hatch.

Driver's position, with handy beer can storage. The Driver's seat has been removed.

External fire extinguisher lever on right hand side.

External fire extinguisher with side skirt mounting bracket in foreground, left hand side.

Final drive mounting bolt detail.

Front left storage bins.

Front roadwheels with sideskirts (bazooka plates).

Fully enclosed cage on opposite side of turret floor is open mesh.

Fume extractor, left hand side.

Gunner's Co-ax firing pedal.

Gunner's elevation and firing controls. Note the cabling and other obstructions that made the turret a H&S nightmare.

Gunner's main sight and Muzzle Reference System light source, and Commander's cupola.

Gunner's main sight housing, from rear.

Gunner's main sight, with armoured cover in closed position.

Gunner's position, with main sight and TOGS viewer in place. Ergonomic design was sadly lacking in Chieftain interiors.

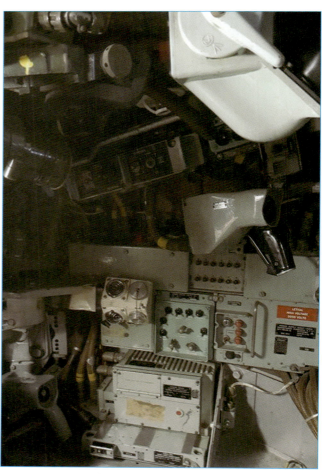

Gunner's seat. A claustrophobic health and safety nightmare.

Headlight brush guard detail.

Idler wheel – note track tension.

Laser sight aperture and chain.

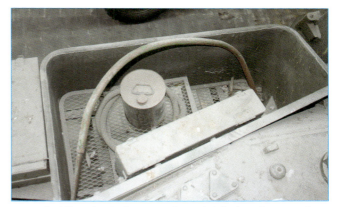

Late style (fully enclosed sides, not mesh) Loader's basket. The rectangular box held flares.

Loader's breech opening lever and safety switch – if the guard was not fully deployed, the gun could not fire.

Loader's hatch from rear.

Loader's position with APFSDS ammo storage. Empty rack above was for two Clansman radios.

Looking forward from turret into the Driver's closed down cab. The large containers on either side are charge bins.

Looking from Loader's to Gunner's position – the green painted tube is the Gunner's emergency sight.

Lower Dozer blade mount Hull Left

Lower Dozer blade mount right.

Main gun breech in closed position with Loader's safety guard partially deployed.

Mounting bracket for storage box on turret (same as rear hull storage boxes).

Mounting for telephone box at rear of tank (removed). Wire to right is telephone cable into tank.

Muzzle Reference System light source from rear.

Muzzle Reference System light source. NOT an auxiliary sight, as sometimes stated.

NBC pack air intake.

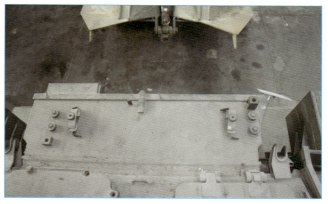

NBC pack from above. The clamps are to hold the camouflage poles used on late Mark Chieftains.

NBC Pack, later type.

Note holes in support for rubber bump stops.

Notek lamp and convoy square.

Overview of Mk 11 turret (with author's car in background)

Overview of turret ,showing Stillbrew and TOGS installations. The chain had a rubber bung on the end used to keep the TLS aperture clean.

Rear bin mounting – note anti-skid on lid.

Rear stowage bin – note size of exhaust pipe.

Rear view – note storage boxes are identical to turret boxes.

Rear view showing brackets for spare track (damaged) and gun clamp, which is hinged.

Return roller detail.

Roadwheel – note hex bolt in end for checking oil level in swing arms.

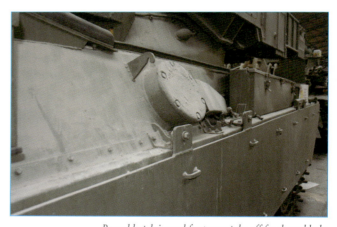

Round hatch is used for power take off for dozer blade.

Rubber guard detail and fuel hatch.

Side view left.

Side view, right.

Sideskirt bracket mounting detail.

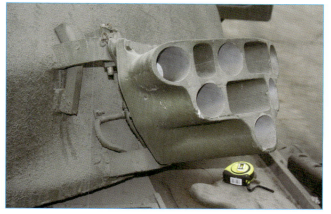

Smoke discharger detail, right hand side.

Stillbrew – detail of cut out for Co-ax.

Stillbrew – detail shot of armour over mantlet with detail of canvas mantlet and Co-ax MG cover.

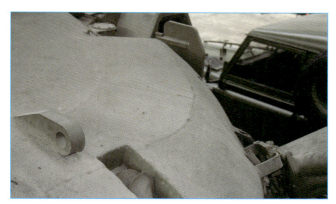

Stillbrew – Right hand side – the outline of the individual boxes which make up Stillbrew can be made out.

Stillbrew armour applique on hull next to Driver's hatch.

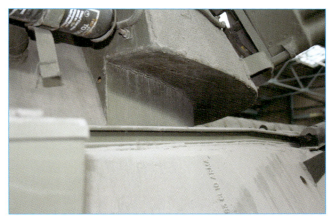

Stillbrew armour from underneath – note how much of the turret ring was unprotected, to allow the turret to traverse the. mounting plate.

Stillbrew armour with cutouts for laser Co-ax and Gunner's main sight.

Stillbrew armour, front left, showing the repositioned smoke discharger.

Stillbrew armour, three-quarter view. The cavity on the left is for the laser sight.

Stillbrew concrete skim was shaped to allow the sight to open.

Stillbrew on left hand turret side.

Suspension mounting detail.

Suspension mounting from underneath hull.

Thermal sleeve covers and fasteners – note the gun clamp pads on this forward section.

TOGS barbette and protection plates.

TOGS barbette door open (TOGS system has been removed). Note simple cable opening system.

TOGS barbette from front with armoured door shut.

TOGS barbette mounting and brackets.

TOGS cooling vent. Note also the mounting bracket for the late style Loader's basket.

TOGS door closed.

TOGS door inside.

TOGS door open with disused antenna base from Larkspur radio in foreground.

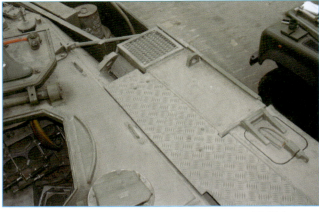

TOGS from rear.

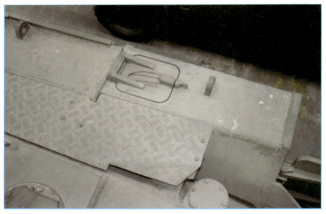

TOGS installation – detail shot of checker plate.

TOGS installation from above. Note checker plate mounted between turret and barbette to prevent trip hazard to crew.

TOGS service door open (The TOGS parts have been removed).

TOGS installation. Side view. Front armoured box holds the TISH (Thermal Imaging Sensor Head). Rear box holds the magic that makes it work.

Top of gun breech – in poor condition.

Track sag – or rather, the lack of! Well adjusted tracks.

TUAM box and fire extingusher mount.

Turret interior, looking towards the Gunner's seat.

View from turret of engine decks – note mesh over engine decks to stop leaves and debris clogging the system.

What's missing – the BV fitted here.

Turret floor under main gun, facing Gunner's position. The racks are for storing HESH rounds and the big blue box is the gunnery computer mounted under the Gunner's seat.

Turret storage box.

View through gap, where Commander's sight should be.

Wiper motors and fixed periscopes of the cupola. Note the join between the cast front and welded rear of the turret, just in front of the cupola.

Willich AVRE

The photographs of the AVRE are a compilation of two vehicles, both part of the same private collection as the Mk 10, and both Gulf War veterans. One vehicle is VOR, but the other is a runner, and has been driven by the Author (and I must say it's a whole lot faster than a standard gun tank without twelve tons of turret on top). Both AVREs currently reside with Tanksalot, but are for sale.

Willich AVRE side view.

Willich AVRE. Top hamper dropped.

Front and side view.

Front view again.

Front view showing Commander's fixed cupola and Driver's position.

Front view.

Aux Gen Engine (same for all Mks).

Crew position RHS of Commander.

Crew seat – one placed each side of Commander's seat. Modified Land Rover seat lever is for raising Commander's seat.

Detail of crude cutting where turret ring was removed.

Detail of front monting for hydraulic ram.

Detail of hydraulic ram to lift top hamper.

Detail of main engine decks (identical to gun tank).

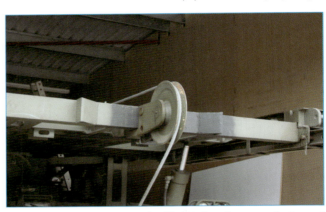

Detail of pulley wheel for winch cable (winch used to recover fascines and roadway after use).

Detail of rear hydraulic ram.

Detail of sliding frame section to allow engine decks to be opened.

Engine decks.

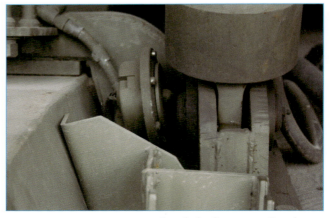

Front hydraulic ram mounting, close up.

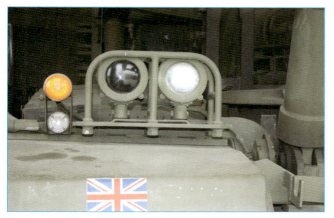

Headlight detail again.

Headlight detail.

Hydraulic and electrical cables to control top frame.

Intricate – and unique to these vehicles – anti-slip coating.

Looking forward over Fascine and roadway carrying frame.

Rear deck and winch detail.

Rear decks again.

Rear decks.

Rear interior detail.

Side view – note aluminium bazooka plate.

Top hamper (front) with extendable bars for recovering fascines.

Top hamper with detail shot of panel which protected the driver from falling pipes and roadway sections.

View from Commander's seat looking forwards into Driver's compartment. Red switch box operates top hamper.

View over top deck.

Winch attachment.

Winch cable drum.

ARRV Mk 7 or CHARRV

Another vehicle from the REME museum reserve collection. A well-used example, needing a fair amount of work to bring it up to museum standard. This vehicle was originally built for the Iranian contract, then taken over as one of the fifty freebies not converted from the original Mk 5 ARV. It remains part of the REME Museum collection.

LH side view – note Atlas 6 ton crane, which was added after experience of Iranian ARRVs.

Rear view. Note reinforced bar on lower hull for towing.

ARRVs were complex vehicles with a mass of additional bracketry welded on the basic Chieftain frame.

Atlas crane – front of jib.

Atlas crane jib from side.

Atlas crane jib.

Atlas crane mount and controls.

Badly bent cable reel holder on rear of vehicle.

Built up section on engine decks for winch motor.

Cable guide mounted on side of engine decks.

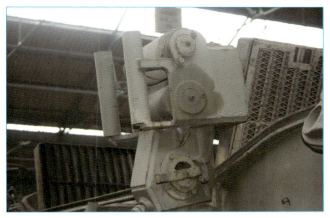

Cable guide.

Cable hitches.

Commander's cupola from rear.

Commander's monocular sight.

Crew access from rear.

Crew access hatch.

Detail of lock nut on dozer blade hydralics.

Dozer blade mount, left hand side.

Dozer blade mount, right hand side.

Engine decks.

Front left corner.

Headlight guard detail.

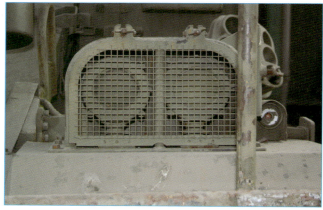

Headlights – with protection against snapped cables.

Heavily modified No. 15 cupola.

Heavy duty dozer blade. Tea kindly provided by museum staff.

Interior of crew position.

Interior detail.

Jerry can stowage on rear side – note holes drilled for drainage.

Left rear.

Dozer blade was specially designed for the vehicle.

Main winch – capable of pulling 90,000 lbs.

One of four smoke dischargers – one on each corner.

Rear stowage – note Challenger 2 prototype in background.

Secondary winch again.

Secondary winch, with crew hatch in background.

Side view of smoke dischargers – note electronic firing cable.

Three quarter view of right rear highlighting unique built up engine deck sides and special stowage for recovery equipment.

Three quarter view right front. Note smoke discharger has more barrels than rear one.

Tool clamp (one each side).

Tool holder on rear.

Tow hitch – another view.

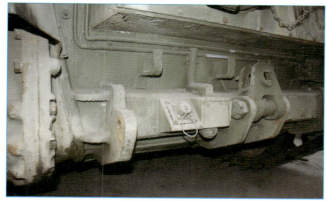

Tow hitch – massively strong, with Notek light and power supply (for trailers).

Underside of drivers hatch.

View from Commander's cupola.

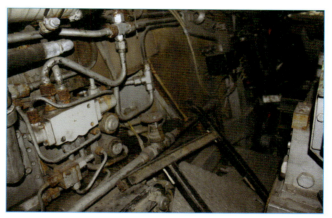

View from Commander's position, looking forward.

View into Commander's position.

View into crew position – very cramped.

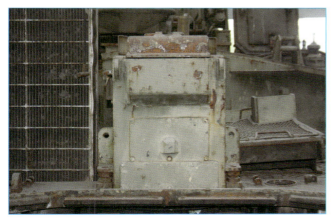

View of rear decks. Tranmission and engine decks are open, radiator is upright, indicating problem with main engine.

View into crew position.

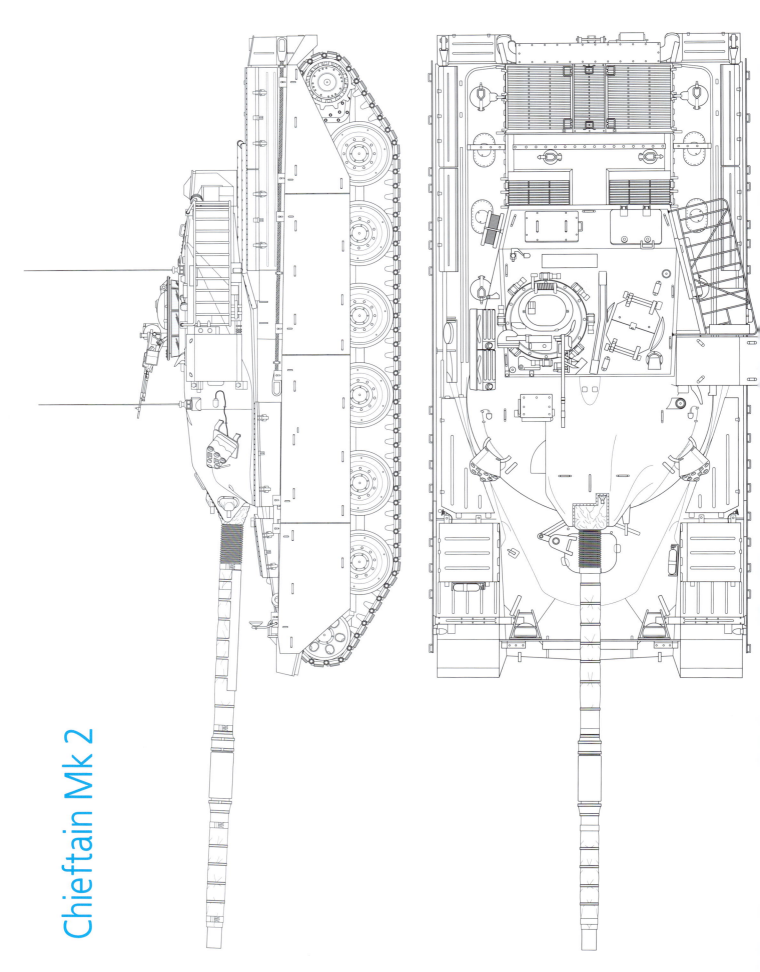

Chieftain Mk 2

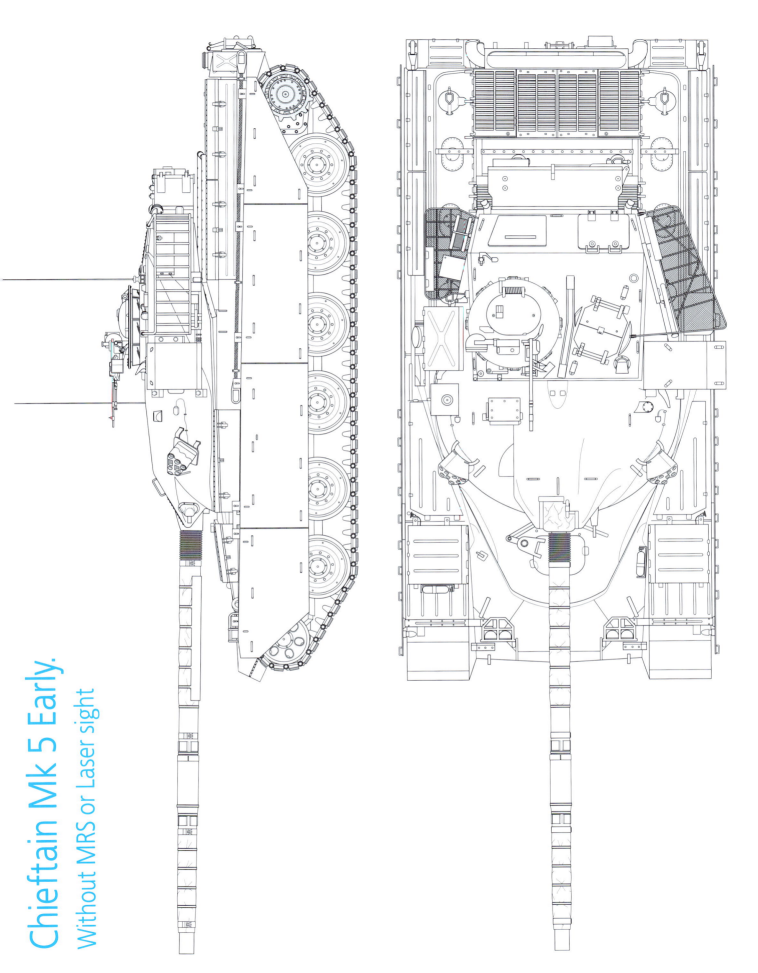

Chieftain Mk 5 Early.
Without MRS or Laser sight

Chieftain Mk 11

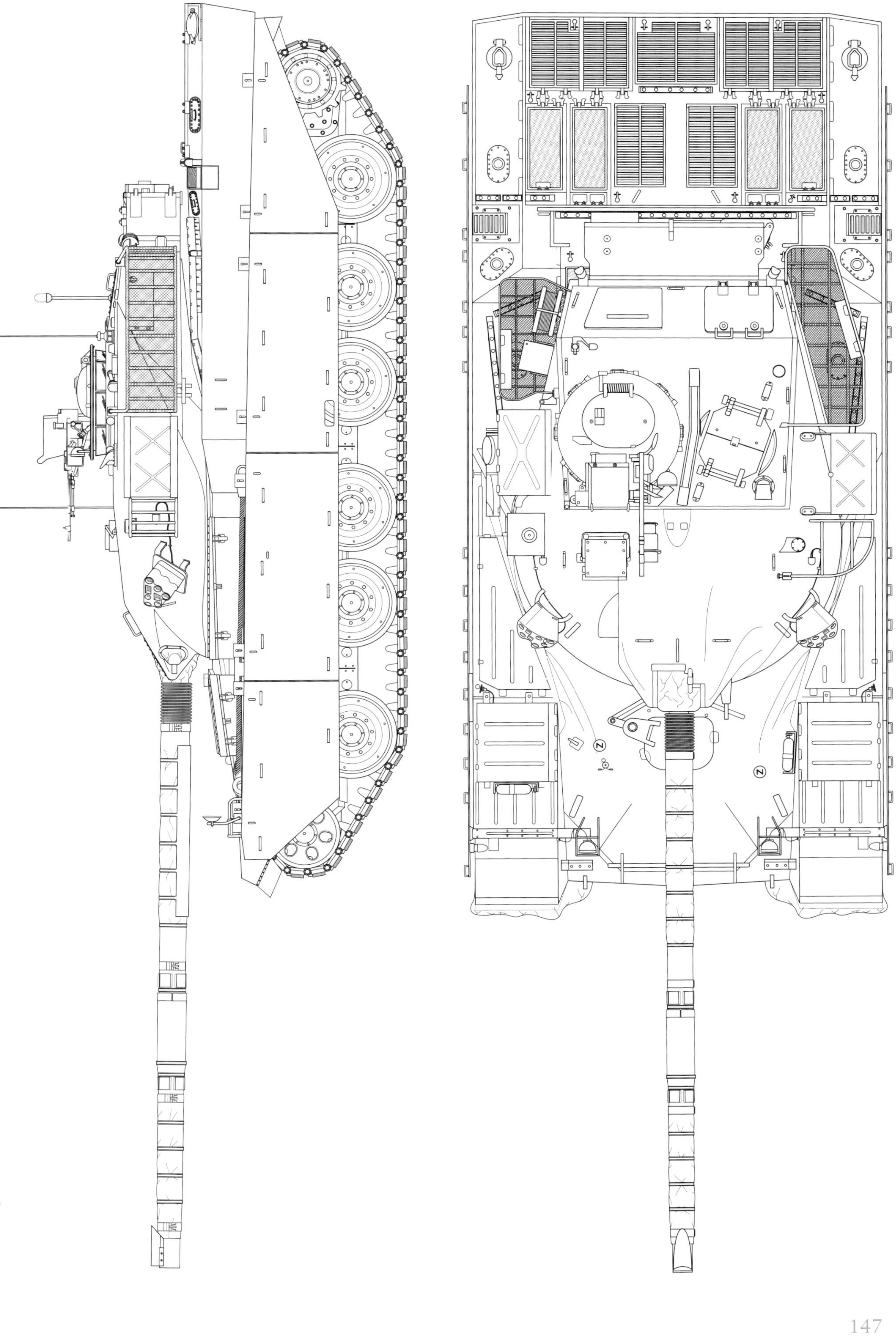

Iraqi Tank Shir

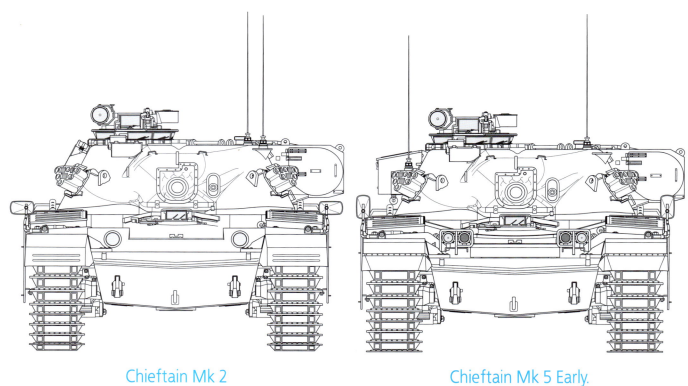

Chieftain Mk 2

Chieftain Mk 5 Early.

Without MRS or Laser sight

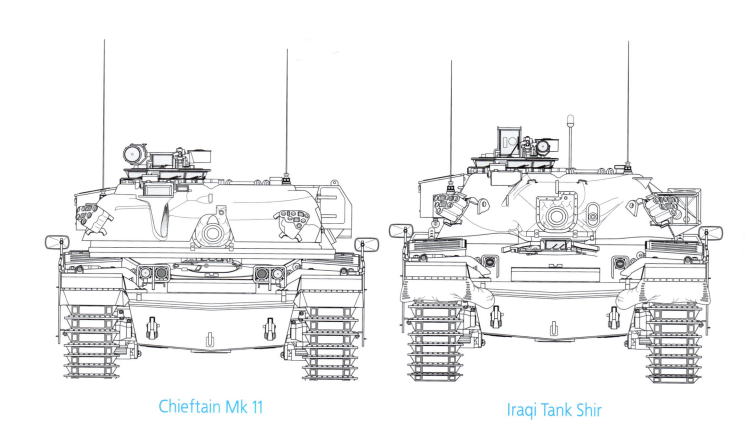

Chieftain Mk 11

Iraqi Tank Shir

Camouflage and Markings, and Notes for Modellers

Standard Colour Schemes

Early Mk 2 Chieftains were delivered from the factory painted in Bronze Green. There is photographic evidence of both the 11th Hussars and 16/5th Lancers having used them in this colour on exercise, and at Hohne Ranges. Late Mk 2s, and all subsequent Chieftains, were delivered in NATO Green, the Black added by the receiving Regiment. The paint was supposed to be Infra-Red Reflective (IRR) and all Chieftains were primed in Red Lead primer (again IRR). The Green and Black camouflage was split approximately two thirds Green, one third Black. There was no "BAOR Standard" scheme, each individual Regiment, and sometimes Squadron or Troop, would devise their own scheme, and apply it.

British tanks of the Cold War era did not carry many markings, usually just the registration plate on the hull front and right rear which was black with white letters, a Bridge Class in a blue (yellow for early chieftains up until the late 1970's) circle to the left of the front number plate, and a tactical sign denoting the vehicle's Squadron, Troop and number within the Troop. These tactical signs developed and changed over the years, but as an example from the 1980s onwards, a yellow Triangle with 32 (three two, not thirty two) inside the triangle would denote A Sqn, 3 Troop, second tank. Some Regiments also had emblems which they would paint on the tanks – the Chinese Eye for 4, and after amalgamation,

RTR Chieftain with a very individual take on the green and black camoflage scheme – spot the swastika. (RK)

RTR Chieftain from a different angle. The green flag means the weapons are safe. (RK)

16 5th Lancers on Hohne ranges. Early Mk 2 still in the bronze green she was delivered in. (RK Collection)

Broken down Chieftain with REME 434 in attendance. Both in field applied winter cam. (Steve O'Connor)

1 RTR, and Regimental Crests for the Cavalry. Regiments, especially the RTR, would name their tanks after each Squadron, using names beginning with its identifying letter (eg, *Defiant* = D Sqn) although there was a tank named *Viscount Montgomery of Alamein*, painted in very small letters!

The Commander's GPMG was a semi-gloss black, not gunmetal finish (as are all GPMGs) and the NATO standard 200 round 7.62 mm ammunition box was chocolate brown, with yellow stencilling. The rounds were brass with gunmetal tips. The disintegrating links which held the rounds together were also brass. The hand held fire extinguishers were bronze green with white stencilling.

Crews would often hide their initials in the scheme or other symbols, even swastikas. 3 RTR had a well-deserved reputation for "interesting" camouflage patterns. Chieftains were painted once or twice a year, initially using spray guns, but later, due to West German environmental laws, paint was applied by hand – officially at least. Unofficially, many Squadrons kept the spray kit, and used it regardless.

The front right bin usually contained rations, and could become very unpleasant with any residue of rotting food. So these bins were often painted gloss white internally, for ease of cleaning, while the other bins remained NATO Green or Red Lead internally.

Arguments still rage about Chieftain having an anti-slip coating. It did – it was called sand – thrown onto wet paint, allowed to dry, and then painted over. The thermal jacket for the main gun was made from canvas, and was never painted. It faded in many unique and interesting ways, so no two Chieftain gun barrels ever looked the same. Internally, all British AFVs of the Cold War era were painted Silver, which never dried, rubbing off onto anything that touched it, and Chieftain was no exception. The thin padding attached to the walls was a dark mustard colour, Humbrol 93 or 94 is a good match, as is Vallejo 70.913 Yellow Ochre. These pads soon became impregnated with ingrained dirt, oil, and assorted filth. Hatches were NATO Green inside, for obvious reasons, but the opening handles could be Post Office Red or JCB Yellow. Seats and hatch pads were various shades of green leather, depending on age and manufacturer. The individual sights were high gloss Bronze Green, as were the Clansman radios. Some internal fitments were White, such as those relating to gun control equipment and NBC air vents, and a variety of other colours were also in evidence.

As previously mentioned, engines and ancillaries were painted a particularly revolting shade of gloss Duck Egg Blue, soon covered in oil. Gearboxes, for some reason, tended to be Bronze Green, but the engine bay itself was Silver, as were the radiators. The armoured engine and gearbox covers were NATO Green inside and out, again, for obvious reasons. Open engine decks with bright silver paint pointing at the sky would have been asking for trouble.

Happy REME fitter (must have been paid in beer) in front of winter camouflaged Chieftain and FV 434. (Steve O'Connor)

Early bronze green Mk 2 reversing off a Mighty Antar tank transporter. (RK Collection)

Mk 3 of the Royal Scots Dragoon Guards, attached to the Berlin Brigade, in an interesting Green on Green scheme. (RK Collection)

Mk 11 of 4 RTR. Note the camo pattern extends under the turret. (Ex Batus vehicle now in private ownership named Lizzie). (Alf van Beem, via Wikimedia Commons)

Two Mk 11s – the one in the foreground has a very unusual three tone camouflage scheme. (RK Collection)

Painted by QRIH in good order for handover day, for an unsuspecting Household Cavalry Officer. Catterick, circa 1989. (Ray Harris)

Painted in gold for a Yell. com ad. (Andy Marshall)

Berlin Brigade

The famous Berlin Urban Camouflage Scheme did not come into use until the mid-1980s. Prior to this, the Berlin Brigade vehicles were painted green and black, like any other tank in BAOR. Officially, the idea for the scheme is credited to Major Clendon Daukes of the 4/7th Dragoon Guards. However, the story told on tank parks is that an Officer on a room inspection saw a Trooper's Tamiya Chieftain model painted in a three-colour brown, grey and white box scheme, acquired the model from the nameless trooper, then a few weeks later, the Berlin scheme appeared. Whichever story is true, the Berlin Urban Camouflage Scheme proved very effective, and actually worked, making a vehicle parked in front of a building harder to see.

Berlin Brigade parade, 18 Jun 1989. (US Dept of Defense, via Wikimedia Commons)

Mk 5 in Berlin urban scheme – out of place in the woods! This is a Mk 5-1, as it has MRS and RMG. (RK)

It was, unsurprisingly, a nightmare to paint, taking three days per tank, one colour per day, with a great deal of masking. The scheme is based on eighteen inch rectangular blocks, using three colours. Chocolate Brown, as used on barracks etc, Light Grey (apparently an RAF colour) and White. This was not bright white, but mixed with whatever was handy to tone it down, including old engine oil. The road wheels were painted Black, or left in Green, depending on who you ask. Engine decks were left Green, as was the hull underside.

Initially, it was only the Chieftains that were painted this way, but it was soon applied to all vehicles in the Berlin Garrison. While using the scheme on APCs and armoured cars was a logical extension, painting four-ton trucks and General Service Land Rovers was not. Whatever the official reasoning for painting *all* the Berlin Brigade vehicles in this scheme, the commonly offered one by those who were there was that it "*looked cool*" to drive around in vehicles painted this way.

The Berlin Brigade tanks were always spotlessly clean, as they had a secondary propaganda and parade role. It was common practice to polish them with diesel fuel-soaked rags, which made them look shiny and clean, but also made the upper surfaces of the tank as slippery as ice, and treacherous to walk on.

Shiny Chieftain Mk 5-3 in Berlin. (RK)

Desert Schemes

Iranian tanks were painted identically to British Chieftains internally, but the external paint was an unusual shade, named *Persian Olive Drab Semi Gloss*. Most which is a very pale light green in reality. Most commercially available paint ranges do not have anything like this colour, but Ammo of Mig Jimenez 929 is a very good match, and can be sprayed or brush painted.

Iranian tanks both before and after the revolution carried very few markings, usually only a roundel in the national colours placed on the bow, each side of the turret and the right rear stowage box. Some vehicles carry the export MS registration, but not all. In the later years of the Iran-Iraq war, wide black, brown or dark green stripes were added to the basic colour. All vehicles became very worn and battered as the conflict progressed.

The surviving Chieftains and new *Mobarez* (*Shir* 1) tanks in Iranian service are now painted in a semi-gloss Desert Yellow, with Bright Green and Light Brown slashes added in a random pattern, which, in the Author's opinion, look like they have been painted by a colour blind child.

Early in the Iran-Iraq War, Iraq captured many Chieftains in full working order, and soon deployed them against their former owners. These were used by regular Iraqi units, and at least thirty were used to equip a unit of Iranian dissidents and deserters, the *Mujaheddin – e-Khaliq* (National Liberation Army). These captured tanks appeared in two distinct schemes. The first, from 1980 to possibly beyond 1982, used the original base colour with the Iranian roundels painted over, and three-figure Arabic numbers in white painted in their place. The front right mudguard had the Iraq green/yellow armour rectangle and "*Army*" or "*National Liberation Army*" in white Arabic script on the front left and right rear mudguards. They also flew large Iraqi flags from at least one antenna. The second scheme was a complete repaint in sand yellow, with random broad bright green (Humbrol Forest Green is a good match) stripes front to back and side to side, very similar to the standard Iraq armour camouflage of the period. These had three-digit numbers on the front hull and each side of the turret. The 'traitor tanks' of the deserter unit had a complex crest design painted on the turret, and below the commander's stowage bin. Many of these tanks had the commander's and possibly the co-axial GPMG replaced with the Russian PKM 7.62 machine gun.

Chieftains sold to Kuwait and Oman were painted in the standard British Mid-Stone desert sand colour. Many companies produce a version of British Mid-Stone, such as Tamiya Desert Yellow XF 59, or Dark Yellow XF 60, Ammo of Mig Jimenez 029 Desert Sand, Model Colour 70847 (123) Dark Sand and Vallejo 71075 Sand. Other manufacturers also have paints that match Mid-Stone, but the Hataka colour is a darker shade, used only on Challenger 2.

Kuwaiti Chieftains had "*The Army*" painted in white Arabic script on the front left and right rear mudguards. During the Gulf War, they also had the coalition black chevron painted on the bazooka plates, although this looked more like a lower case 'n' than the standard chevron, and with three vertical white lines behind the chevron, the purpose of which is unknown. Pennants in Kuwaiti colours were flown from the radio antennae.

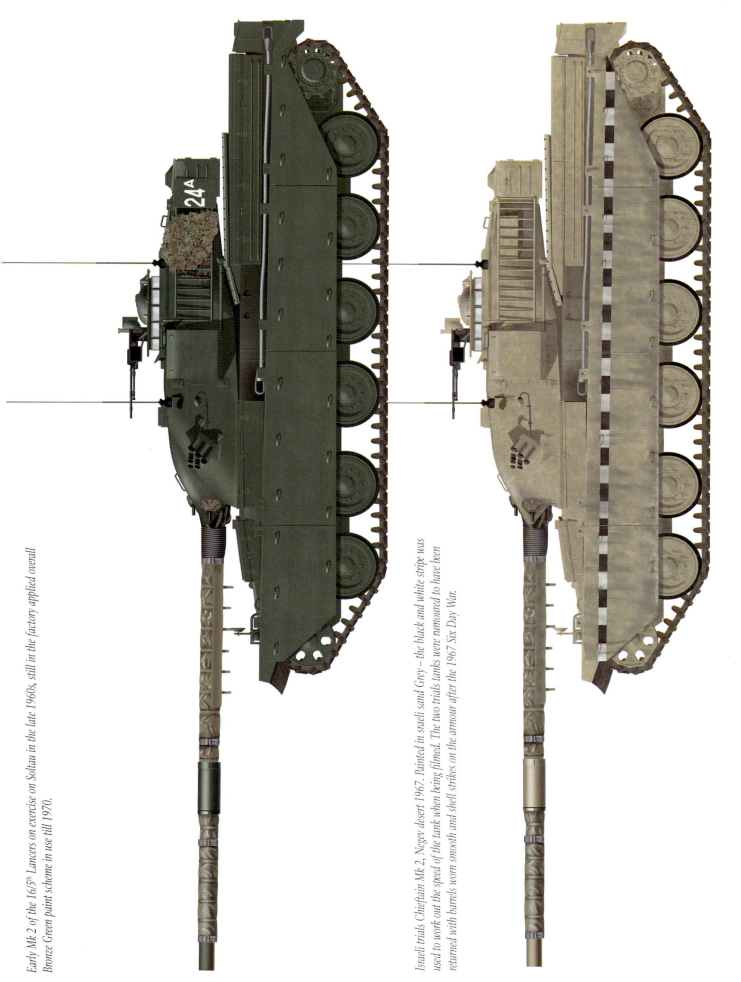

Early Mk 2 of the 16/5th Lancers on exercise on Soltau in the late 1960s, still in the factory applied overall Bronze Green paint scheme in use till 1970.

Israeli trials Chieftain Mk 2, Negev desert 1967. Painted in sraeli sand Grey – the black and white stripe was used to work out the speed of the tank when being filmed. The two trials tanks were rumoured to have been returned with barrels worn smooth and shell strikes on the armour after the 1967 Six Day War.

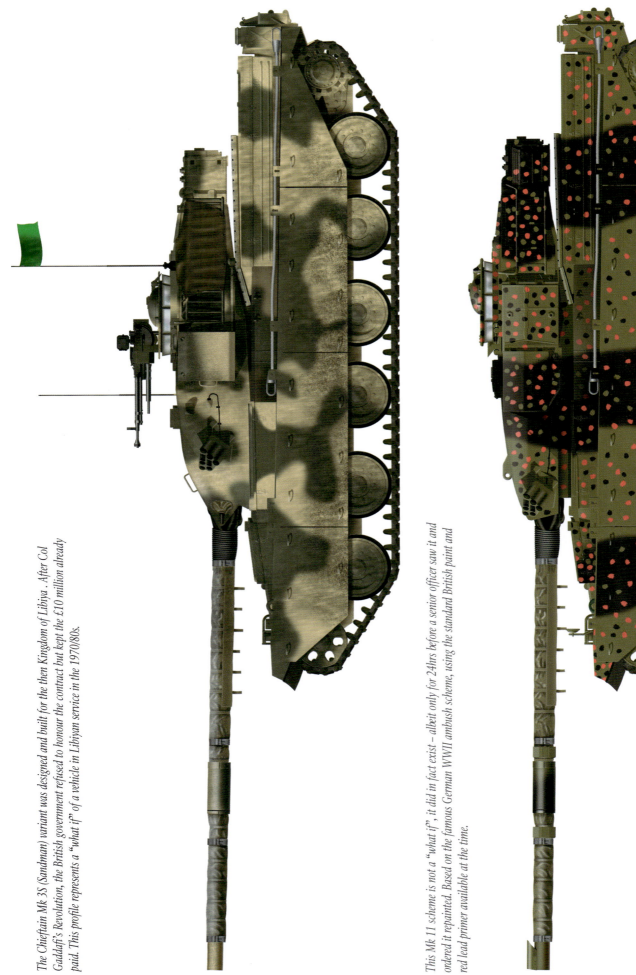

The Chieftain Mk 3S (Sandman) variant was designed and built for the then Kingdom of Libiya. After Col Gaddafi's Revolution, the British government refused to honour the contract but kept the £10 million already paid. This profile represents a "what if" of a vehicle in Libiyan service in the 1970/80s.

This Mk 11 scheme is not a "what if", it did in fact exist – albeit only for 24hrs before a senior officer saw it and ordered it repainted. Based on the famous German WWII ambush scheme, using the standard British paint and red lead primer available at the time.

The Israeli Mk 4. Two of these tanks were built and ROF Leeds and Vickers in Newcastle were ready to go into full production when the British Goverment cancelled the deal. The two Mk 4s had steel tracks, built up sides for extra fuel and a different road wheel layout. This profile represents a "what if" Mk 4 in Israeli service.

Chieftain Mk 11 movie star, used in the film "Reign of Fire". This privately owned vehicle was dressed for the film with a DSHK cannon, speakers and a battery of car spotlights, then sprayed in watered down black paint to represent charring.

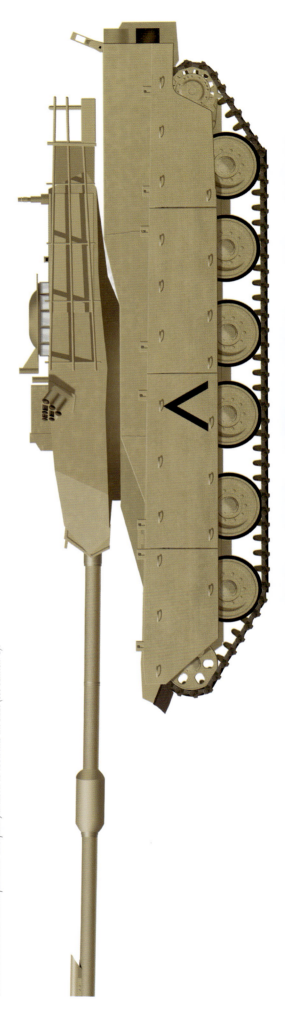

"ChiefBrams" – The US armed forces will not supply current equipment to movie makers, so any M1 Abrams seen in the movies will in fact be a Chieftain, dressed to look like an M1. (see Annex C).

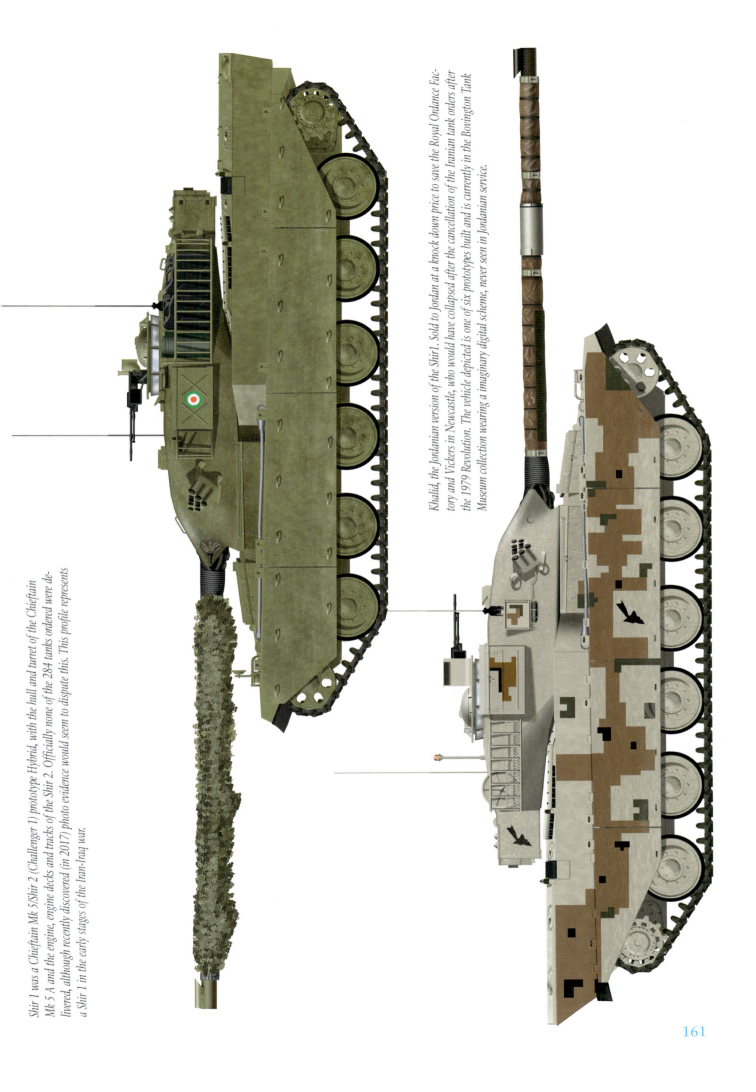

Shir 1 was a Chieftain Mk 5/Shir 2 (Challenger 1) prototype Hybrid, with the hull and turret of the Chieftain Mk 5 A and the engine, engine decks and tracks of the Shir 2. Officially none of the 284 tanks ordered were delivered, although recently discovered (in 2017) photo evidence would seem to dispute this. This profile represents a Shir 1 in the early stages of the Iran-Iraq war.

Khalid, the Jordanian version of the Shir1. Sold to Jordan at a knock down price to save the Royal Ordance Factory and Vickers in Newcastle, who would have collapsed after the cancellation of the Iranian tank orders after the 1979 Revolution. The vehicle depicted is one of six prototypes built and is currently in the Bovington Tank Museum collection wearing a imaginary digital scheme, never seen in Jordanian service.

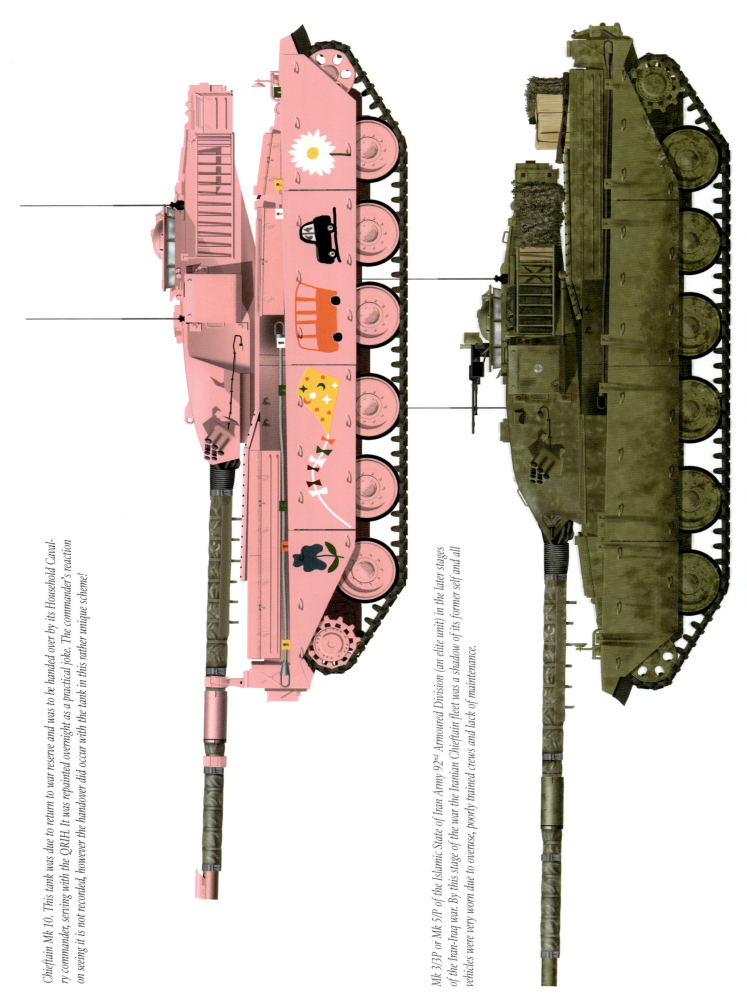

Chieftain Mk 10. This tank was due to return to war reserve and was to be handed over by its Household Cavalry commander, serving with the QRIH. It was repainted overnight as a practical joke. The commander's reaction on seeing it is not recorded, however the handover did occur with the tank in this rather unique scheme!

Mk 3/3P or Mk 5/P of the Islamic State of Iran Army 92nd Armoured Division (an elite unit) in the later stages of the Iran-Iraq war. By this stage of the war the Iranian Chieftain fleet was a shadow of its former self and all vehicles were very worn due to overuse, poorly trained crews and lack of maintenance.

Mk 5/1 of 3 RTR. 3 RTR had a well deserved reputation for "unusual" camouflage schemes, spot the swastika hidden in the scheme. The profile shows the Chieftain racing Wolfgang to the Overnight RV on the infamous Soltau training area.

At the end of the Iran-Iraq war the Iranians were estimated to have 250–350 Chieftains left in service, some of which are still in service today. This profile is taken from a photo secretly taken during a military parade of "new" military equipment somewhere in Iran.

Mk 5/4 unknown unit, BAOR West Germany late 1970s/early 1980s. It is in the NATO Green and Black scheme adopted in 1970-71. The large red rectangle and lack of bazooka plates show a vehicle acting as OPFOR (Opposing Forces) during one of the large scale field exercises conducted in the cold war era.

One of many captured and stripped Iranian Chieftains discovered amongst the huge vehicle graveyard outside Bagdad, after the 2003 invasion.

Mk 10 of the 11th Hussars attached to the Berlin Brigade in the famous (or infamous if you had to paint it), very effective Berlin Urban Scheme. The profile has been created from the original template, a copy of which is in the Author's possession.

Oman was leased 15 refurbished Mk 7s from British Army stocks and later purchased another 15, the last Chieftains built before the production line closed in 1985. This Chieftain was written of during an amphibious landing exercise, when it was driven off the LST too far from the beach and flooded. The tank is painted using the British BATUS scheme colours.

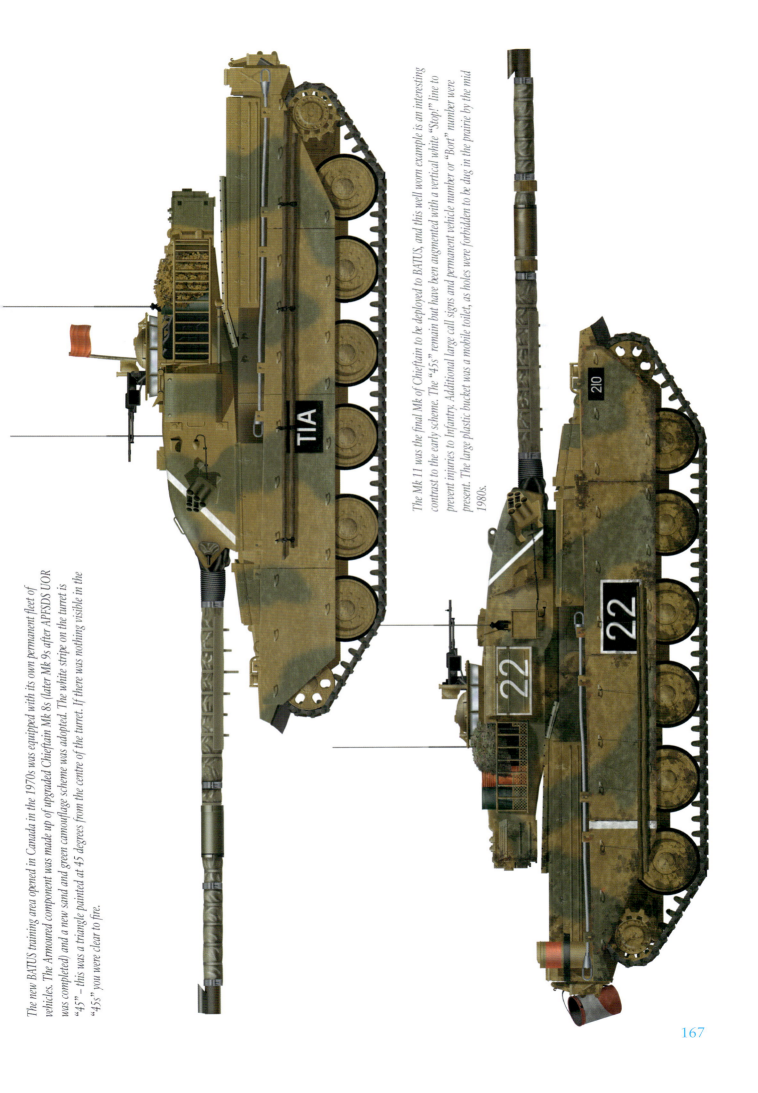

The new BATUS training area opened in Canada in the 1970s was equipped with its own permanent fleet of vehicles. The Armoured component was made up of upgraded Chieftain Mk 8s (later Mk 9s after APFSDS UOR was completed) and a new sand and green camouflage scheme was adopted. The white stripe on the turret is "45" – this was a triangle painted at 45 degrees from the centre of the turret. If there was nothing visible in the "45s" you were clear to fire.

The Mk 11 was the final Mk of Chieftain to be deployed to BATUS, and this well worn example is an interesting contrast to the early scheme. The "45s" remain but have been augmented with a vertical white "Stop!" line to prevent injuries to Infantry. Additional large call signs and permanent vehicle number or "Bort" number were present. The large plastic bucket was a mobile toilet, as holes were forbidden to be dug in the prairie by the mid 1980s.

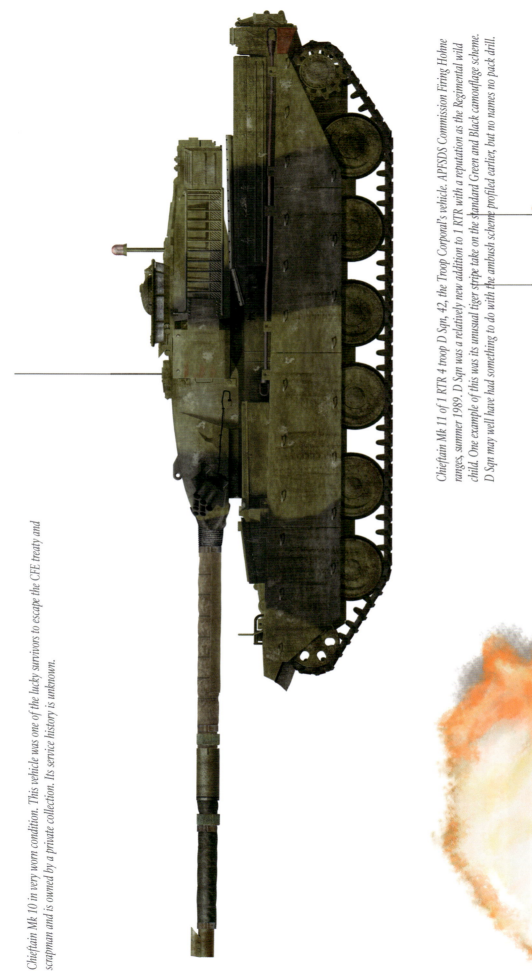

Chieftain Mk 10 in very worn condition. This vehicle was one of the lucky survivors to escape the CFE treaty and scrapman and is owned by a private collection. Its service history is unknown.

Chieftain Mk 11 of 1 RTR 4 troop D Sqn, 42, the Troop Corporal's vehicle. APFSDS Commission Firing Holme ranges, summer 1989. D Sqn was a relatively new addition to 1 RTR with a reputation as the Regimental wild child. One example of this was its unusual tiger stripe take on the standard Green and Black camouflage scheme. D Sqn may well have had something to do with the ambush scheme profiled earlier, but no names no pack drill.

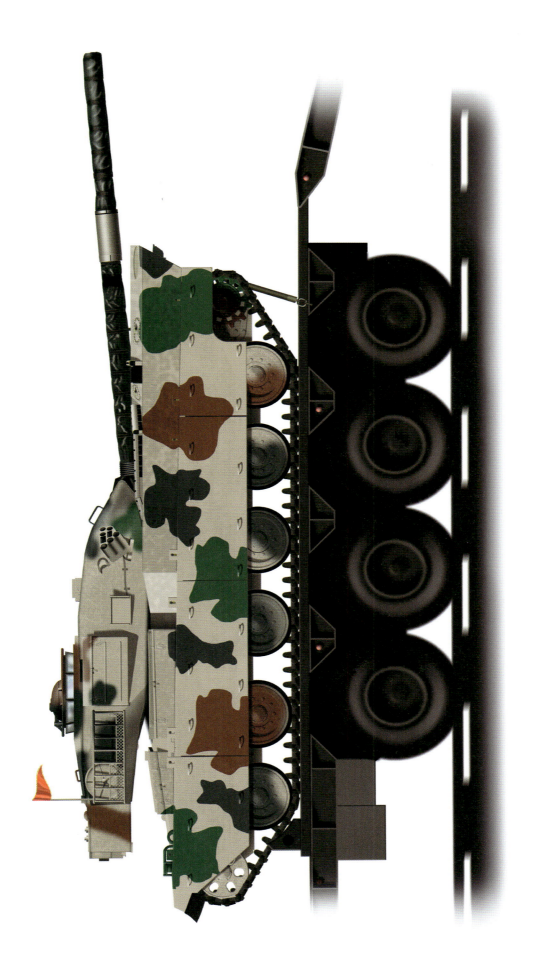

Iranian Shir 1 in service today profile based on Clandestine photo taken on an active Iranian military base.

Stripped down Iranian Mk 3 with much of its standard equipment missing after "upgrading" in the state armament factory, where a Russian T-72 V12 Diesel engine was supposedly installed.

Chieftain 800/900. An unsuccessful attempt to upgrade Chieftain with a down-rated CV 12 (Challenger) engine and Chobham armour. At least two vehicles were built and much promotional material printed but no orders were forthcoming. One vehicle survives.

Chieftain Mk 11 of D Sqn 1RTR charging down the pylon line on the Soltau Training area after the exercise has finished. Note the level of filth from two weeks on exercise. The additional stowage including CVR(T) Scorpion rear bin and definitely non-tactical blue plastic NAFFI washing bowl.

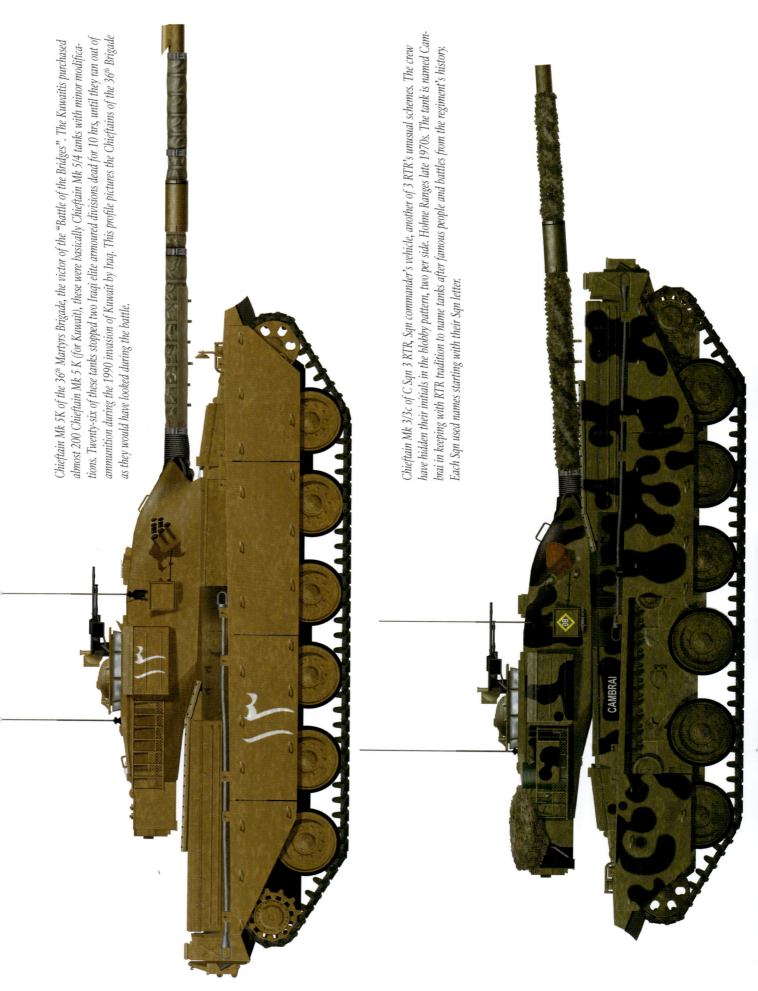

Chieftain Mk 5K of the 36th Martyrs Brigade, the victor of the "Battle of the Bridges". The Kuwaitis purchased almost 200 Chieftain Mk 5 K (for Kuwait), these were basically Chieftain Mk 5/4 tanks with minor modifications. Twenty-six of these tanks stopped two Iraqi elite armoured divisions dead for 10 hrs, until they ran out of ammunition during the 1990 invasion of Kuwait by Iraq. This profile pictures the Chieftains of the 36th Brigade as they would have looked during the battle.

Chieftain Mk 3/3c of C Sqn 3 RTR, Sqn commander's vehicle, another of 3 RTR's unusual schemes. The crew have hidden their initials in the blobby pattern, two per side. Hohne Ranges late 1970s. The tank is named Cambrai in keeping with RTR tradition to name tanks after famous people and battles from the regiment's history. Each Sqn used names starting with their Sqn letter.

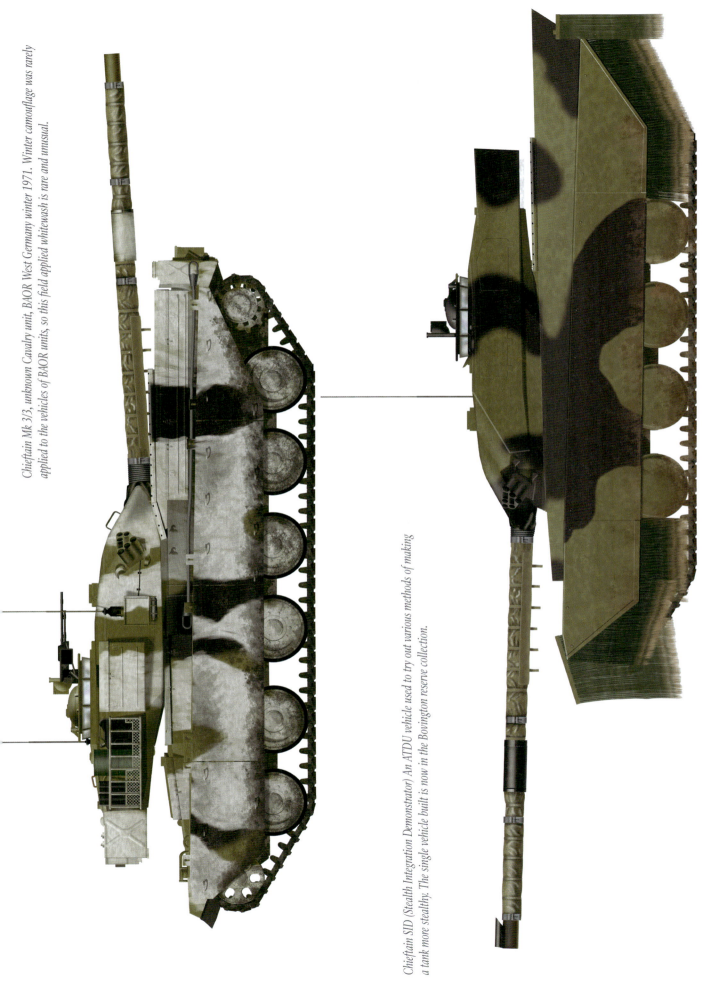

Chieftain Mk 3/3, unknown Cavalry unit, BAOR West Germany winter 1971. Winter camouflage was rarely applied to the vehicles of BAOR units, so this field applied whitewash is rare and unusual.

Chieftain SID (Stealth Integration Demonstrator) An ATDU vehicle used to try out various methods of making a tank more stealthy. The single vehicle built is now in the Bovington reserve collection.

JagdChieftain Concept Vehicle. Modelled after the Jagdpanzers and Stugs used by the Germans in WWII, this ultimately pointless vehicle always grabs the imagination of anyone who sees it. The profile is a "what if" of an operational Jagdchieftain, stalking its prey across the Soltau Training area.

Selected Preserved Examples

The end for the Chieftain came quite swiftly, and many tanks were destroyed as part of the CFE (Conventional Forces Europe) treaty terms, or smelted down by the scrapman. Others were (and still are) used as hard targets on various ranges in the UK and abroad.

An unusually large number of Chieftains have survived as gate guardians, or in private hands. Bovington has the largest single collection, from prototypes to Mk 11s and special purpose vehicles, which it either displays or retains for exchanges with other museums, or is holding in its reserve collection.

Listed below are some of the survivors. This is by no means a comprehensive list, but a selection of where you can see, and in some places, get rides on, or even drive, the fantastic beast that is the Chieftain.

Displayed and Preserved Chieftains Listing (not exhaustive) – 2018

Country	Location	Establishment	Notes
Australia	Cairns, North Queensland	Australian Armour and Artillery Museum	Mk 10 in black/green camouflage.
Belgium	Brasschaat	Belgian Tank Museum	Mk 10 in black/green camouflage.
Canada	Fort McMurray, Alberta	Jack Cross Collection – Armourcrossalberta.com	Mk 10 in black/green camouflage, named 'Alberta Crude'. Displayed locally.
			Mk 11 in desert scheme, named 'Melissa'.
	Ottawa	Canadian War Museum	Ex-BATUS Mk 11.
	Suffield	BATUS	A large number of abandoned Chieftains, AVLBs and AVREs are lined up along the main boundary road, on public view.
			Mk 11 on display outside HQ Building.
China	Beijing	China North Vehicle Research Institute	Likely ex-Iranian Mk 5 – battle damage noted.
Czech Republic	Lešany	Military Technical Museum	Running exhibit. (Ex-Iranian or Kuwait, captured Iraq, then via Jordan).
France	Saumur	Musée des Blindés	Berlin Brigade scheme.
Germany	Sennelager	Normandy Barracks	Displayed within Barracks.
Iran	Tehran	Holy Defense Museum	Outdoor exhibit.
Israel	Latrun	Yad La-Shiryon Tank Museum	Outdoor exhibit.
Jordan	Amman	Royal Tank Museum	Mk 3 Chieftain (ex Iran?) in green and brown "British" scheme.
			FV 4030/2 Khalid (digital Camo).
New Zealand	Huntly, Waikato District, North Island	Des Sullivan – private collection	Mk 10 in original Berlin Scheme. Viewing by arrangement.
Oman	Muscat	Sultan's Armed Forces Museum	Mk 7/2 on external display in immaculate condition.
	Shafa	Shafa Camp	Two Mk 5 or Mk 7 in hull down positions flanking gate fort towers.
Poland	Bydgoszcz	Land Forces Museum	Exchanged by Bovington for running T-72.
Russia	Kubinka	Tank Museum	Iranian Mk 3 or 5 – large section of glacis armour cut out, (test?) shell strikes evident.
Sweden	Strängnäs	Swedish Tank Museum (Arsenalen)	Mk 10, in very good running condition.

USA	Fort Benning, GA	National Armor and Cavalry Museum (not yet built)	Held in Sand Hill storage facility, within the active base, for the foreseeable future. Prototype, updated to Mk 1 standard – former West German exchange example.
	Las Vegas, NV	Battlefieldvegas.com	Film hire 'Chiefbrams' – can be hired for car crushing.
	Mesa, AZ	Neal Bros, Bulletproof Diesel	Painted in (non-authentic for Gun Chieftain) Op Granby Challenger desert scheme.
	Santa Clarita, CA and Fayetteville, GA	Armytrucks Inc.	Film hire 'Chiefbrams' – two on offer – one originally green, both now in sand scheme.
	Stow, MA	Collings Foundation JML Collection, American Heritage Museum.	Moved from Jacques Littlefield Collection in Palo Alto, CA to American Heritage Museum, currently under construction. Desert scheme with mineclearing blade (Iran-Iraq-Jordan(?)).
	Uvalde, TX	Drivetanks.com	Mk 6 – can be hired for car crushing.
UK	Aldershot, Hants	Military Museum	Outdoor exhibit, alongside Challenger.
	Ancaster, Lincs	Ancaster Kart Racing	Roadside exhibit.
	Ashchurch, Gloucs	Defence Storage and Distribution Agency	Gate Guard – can be seen from A46 road.
			Former second gate guard – AVRE currently under restoration.
	Bailey Down, Nr Winchester, Hants	Juniper Leisure	Tank driving/rides on modified Mk 10 (rear of turret removed).
	Bovington, Dorset	Tank Museum – Main Halls	Mk 11.
			Mk 11 (captioned Mk 12) turret can be accessed when volunteers present.
		Tank Museum – Reserve Collection	'Boudicca' Mk 11 Running exhibit.
			Mk 11 formerly REME reserve collection. Now used as Bovington reference Chieftain.
			Mk 10 with mine plough fitted. Displayed alongside access road, outside the Reserve Collection hangar.
			Chieftain SID – kept in running condition, in good overall condition.
			Crazy Horse – in poor condition and deteriorating. Urgently in need of restoration.
			Prototype G7 (marked G1 on turret) in good condition. Non runner.
			Prototype P6 saved from scrapyard, in poor condition.
			40 Ton Centurion – in good condition. Another turret on external display, fitted with 140 mm experimental gun.
			Mk 10 returned from loan at Bucks railway museum, stored externally. In poor condition.
			FV 4211 Aluminium Chieftain. Non-runner, hidden at rear of Reserve Collection.
			Chieftain 800 (named 900 but 900 known destroyed) good condition but no engine installed.
			JagdChieftain CTR – stored without false gun.
			FV 4030/2 Shir 1/Khalid in fake Jordanian Digital scheme. Currently a non runner.
		Allenby Barracks Armour Centre	Two Chieftains, Mks unknown. Gate Guards.
		Armoured Trials and Development Unit	Gate Guard.
	Catterick, N Yorks	Cambrai Barracks	Mk 11 Gate Guard.
		Infantry Training Centre	Mk 11 Gate Guard – very poor condition (possible restoration in future).
	Colsterworth, Lincs	Witham (Specialist Vehicles) Ltd	Chieftain 2000 noted in yard.
			Shed full of ex-war reserve Mk 10s. Denied by Witham's, but seen by Author!
	Dudley, West Midlands	Delph Hill Industrial Estate, Brierly Hill	Mk 10 – In car park, facing road.
	Finchingfield, Essex	Undisclosed	Recovered from field for intended restoration – used to look like a bush!
	Fornham St Peter, Norfolk	Norfolk Tank Museum	Turbine Chieftain CTE now with original L60 fitted – running exhibit.
	Helmdon, Northants	Tanks A Lot	Running exhibit. Can be ridden.
			Mk 10. For sale. Running condition, new paint, but poor mechanically.
			Willich AVRE in running condition – For sale.
			Willich AVRE in running condition – For sale.

UK	Husbands Bosworth, Leics	Armourgeddon	Running exhibit. Can be ridden.
	Lulworth Camp & Range, Dorset	Gunnery School	Mk 11 Gate Guard – inaccessible to public.
		Ranges	Numerous Chieftains used as hard targets – occasional public access.
	Lyneham, Wilts	REME Reserve Collection	CHARRV. In storage at RAF Lyneham.
	Maldon, Essex	Combined Services Military Museum	Berlin Bde Mk 10, outdoor exhibit.
	New Forest, Hants	Undisclosed	2 x Mk 10 and Mk 7 ARRV, in private ownership.
	Portsmouth, Hants	Fort Southwick, Portsdown Hill	Mk 10. Bazooka plates and turret fittings removed.
	Pembroke, Wales	Castlemartin Ranges	Gate Guard. Can be viewed from public road.
	Shrivenham, Wilts	Defence College of Management and Technology	One of several tanks in a non-public instructional collection.
	Warrington, Cheshire	RHQ 75 Engr Regt (V)	Gate Guard – AVRE.
	Winchester	Sir John Moore Barracks	Mk 10 Gate Guard.
	Weybourne, Norfolk	Muckleburgh Collection	Running exhibit.
			Indicates no public access.

Annex C
Hollywood Waits
at the End of the Rainbow...

Besides tanks, your humble Author also has a keen interest in Sci-Fi, and that sort of thing. Which leads on to this fun listing.

The Chieftain has had a surprising number of appearances in TV and film over the years, sometimes as itself, and other times made to look like another tank. Most notably in recent years, it has appeared many times as the M1 Abrams, a tank it was – in this Author's opinion – superior to in almost every way, except the lack of Chobham armour!

Sadly, due to tedious copyright issues (TV and film companies would doubtless want *lots* of money) no photographs from the movies can be included here, but there is always the internet to look up. For added interest, a couple of photos have been included. The list is not exhaustive, and I would love to know if anyone spots the old girl in any movie or TV series not listed here.

Goldeneye (1995).

Salisbury Uriah Heep (1971) Chieftain's first foray into popular culture was an album cover, featuring a Mk 2 emerging from orange smoke. The original LP had a gatefold sleeve, with a photo of the underside of a Chieftain overhanging a ridge on the inside, with the turret facing rearwards.

Die Hamburger Krankheit (1979) German dystopian film. A mysterious disease claims several lives in Hamburg. A standard camo Chieftain has a roll-on part, as the characters make their way to safety in the Bavarian Alps.

Mr Bean (1994) In the episode '*Back to School, Mr Bean*', a Chieftain squashes his Mini at a school fete.

Goldeneye (1995) Four Chieftains are made up to look like T-55s. All these tanks still exist – the three background tanks are being restored to original service condition. The "hero" tank is seen being driven by *007*. This one is still in full film make-up, and was returned from Northern Ireland to the UK mainland in 2017. Interestingly, all four tanks were originally converted for the MOD by an effects company, to act as OPFOR vehicles on Salisbury Plain.

One Foot in the Grave (1995) Episode 33 – '*The Exterminating Angel*' – A Chieftain squashes a Jaguar car in a very contrived scene, to allow the catch phrase to be repeated.

Sgt Bilko (1996) Chieftain as M1 appears in background of several scenes, with the main character played by Steve Martin.

Courage Under Fire (1996) Chieftains (although some say Centurions, but I don't think so) stand in for M1s. A lot is seen of these tanks – at least three separate vehicles are used, and are central to the lead character's story.

Steel (1997) Superhero movie. Fake M1 makes an appearance. Critically panned. Cost $17M, but takings only $1.6M.

Malcolm in the Middle (2000 – 2006) Chieftain disguised as an M1 appears in several episodes.

Reign of Fire (2002) Matthew McConaughey's character is seen riding atop a Mk 11, fitted with a Soviet DSHK Heavy Machine Gun and lots of other dragon-slaying greeblies! It appeared in several scenes of the movie, before being destroyed in a blaze of dragonfire towards the end of the film.

Hulk (2003) In the original *Hulk* movie, at least two Chieftains act as an M1.

Cradle to the Grave (2003) Background as M1.

Jarhead (2005) In several scenes, standing in for the M1.

Children of Men (2006) A Chieftain Mk 10 in an interesting Green/Black Digital urban camouflage appears towards the end of the film, in the refugee camp, alongside a similarly painted CVR(T) Scorpion.

Southland Tales (2006) Background, as M1.

Jericho (2006) American post-apocalyptic TV series. In background in many episodes, as yes you guessed it, an "M1".

D-War (2007) Terrible film from South Korea! Chieftain as M1 in background.

The Kingdom (2007) Background, as an M1. Again.

The Day The Earth Stood Still (Remake, 2008) Chieftain as an M1 guarding the GORT spacecraft when it lands. Also, when GORT transforms into the scouring nanites, several Chieftain M1 lookalikes are disintegrated in the beginning of the final scenes.

Cloverfield (2008) Background as M1 ...but gets to fire its gun in one scene!

Iron Man (2008) Background as, yes, you guessed it, an M1.

Zombieland (2009) Apocalyptic comedy horror. (?) Background as M1 – whoever owns the Chieftain M1 lookalike is making a good living from it! (ArmyTrucks Inc., proud suppliers to the movie industry, have two of them...)

The Walking Dead (Series 1, 2010) The lead character shelters from zombies, inside a Chieftain made to look like an M1, and the tank appears as background in several other episodes.

Battle: Los Angeles (2011) Background, as an M1.

Red Dawn (Remake, 2012) In several scenes, including a couple of battles as an M1.

Ozombie (aka Osombie) (2012) Bin Laden is back from the dead, and creating a zombie army. Possibly THE worst film ever made – yes, worse even than *Battlefield Earth*, or (thankfully not a Chieftain) *Tank 432*. This utter dreck features a 'Chiefbrams' on the cover of the DVD and in the movie (which has open hatches – but the crew are ashamed to show their faces).

Fast and Furious 6 (2013) Chieftain made up to look like, well I don't really know – a sort of Sci-Fi tank! At least it's not an Abrams... Bursts out of a truck onto the road (this was actually filmed – this was not CGI). Then proceeds to keep up with various racing cars, while committing various death-defying stunts. Absolutely hysterical to watch.

Godzilla (US remake, 2014) Firing at Godzilla from Golden Gate Bridge to no effect, then destroyed by Godzilla. Again made to look like an M1.

Doctor Who (Series 9, Episode 1, 2015) Peter Capaldi as the Doctor makes a 'grand entrance' on a desert-painted Mk 10.

'Uma Thurman' by Fall Out Boy (2015) Pop video. Ends with a 'M1' titled 'UMA' crushing a pickup truck.

Fast and Furious 6 (2013).

Fantastic Four (aka 'Fant4stic') (2015) Chieftain in a Marvel Comics superhero movie, identifiable by the six roadwheels and 'U' shape on the glacis. What's more, winner of three awards! Unfortunately, these were *Golden Raspberries* (Razzies) for Worst Picture (tied), Worst Director, Worst Prequel, Remake, Rip-off or Sequel – but it couldn't have been that bad, failing to win Worst Screen Combo or Worst Screenplay, for which it was nominated.

Not discouraged by this setback…

Transformers – The Last Knight (2017) Chieftain's latest appearance on film. Nominated for no less than nine *Razzies* in 2018, for Worst Picture, Worst Actor, Worst Supporting Actor (two nominations), Worst Supporting Actress, Worst Screen Combo, Worst Remake, Rip-off or Sequel, Worst Director, and Worst Screenplay. Thankfully, it seems nobody had anything bad to say about the tank – beyond, maybe… '*Haven't I seen that somewhere before?*'

While at least one 'Chiefbrams' has been offered for hire in a green scheme, most if not all, now appear in desert sand. Which is where all the action (and money) is at. *And why not? Who cares what it's about, as long as the kids go..!* It seems more than likely that these were ex-BATUS vehicles, hastily disposed of by Defence Sales at bargain prices, to eager American buyers. But, to be fair, who'd have thought it? Certainly not the long-suffering British Army tank crews, who tolerated the high-maintenance, temperamental girl – who would later become a movie star! Or, as the Guardian might put it – *Best Female Actor…*

The L24 Armour Piercing Fin Stabilised Discarding Sabot (APFSDS) round in flight as the Sabots peel away. An extremely deadly round, the rhyme on the tank park went "Freddie Fin he f***s everyFin". (RK Collection)

Specifications

Combat weight: 55 to 62 tons, depending on Mark
Overall length: 10.8 m (35 ft 5.2 in) gun forward
Hull length: 7.5 m (24 ft 7.3 in) From Mk 2 onwards
Height: 2.9 m (9 ft 6.2 in)
Width: 3.5 m (11 ft 5.8 in)
Powerplant: Leyland L60 (diesel, multi-fuel compression ignition) from 695 bhp (518 kW) in Mk 2 to
    750 bhp in Mk 11 (L60 version 14a)
Range: 500 km (310 mi)
Maximum road speed: 48 km/h (28 mph)
Cross-country speed: 30 km/h (23 mph)
Armour: turret front, 195 mm (7.7 in) RHA (60°) Stillbrew up armouring package on Mk 10 and Mk 11
    increased this. Exact specification is unavailable

Armament

120 mm L11A5 rifled tank gun
Rate of fire: 10 rounds per minute for the first minute and 6 thereafter.
Elevation: – 10 to +20 degrees
Laser rangefinder from Mk 5/2 onwards.
Coaxial L8A1 7.62 mm machine gun
Cupola-mounted L37A1 7.62 mm machine gun
Mark 1 to Mark 5/1 models had a coaxial Browning M2 .50-inch (12.7 mm) ranging machine gun prior
    to the introduction of the laser rangefinder.

Equipment

Twin Clansman VRC 353 VHF Radio sets (1979 onward)
1 C42 1 B47 Larkspur VHF radios (pre 1979)
2 x six-barrel smoke grenade dischargers
Bulldozer blade (optional – fitted to one tank per squadron)

About the Author

The Author is a life-long tank modeller (which, alas, doesn't mean he's any good at it) and has been fascinated with tanks and military history since he was a boy.

He joined 1 RTR in the late 1980s, at the end of the Cold War, where he rose to the dizzying heights of Regimental Modeller, this coveted Secondary Duty providing a career high! (Best job he ever had – no-one else in the Regiment made models!)

At this time, 1 RTR was equipped with the Mk 11 Chieftain, and it is here that the Author developed his passion for the big, smelly, dirty and unreliable beast, and began his research.

Since leaving the Forces, he has maintained his interest in military history, and the Chieftain in particular, and has had many articles published in the modelling press. He also works closely with a well-known model company and has been successful in encouraging new models of the Chieftain and other Cold War British subjects to be produced as high quality plastic model kits.

Glossary

APC	Armoured Personnel Carrier
APFSDS	Armour Piercing Fin Stabilised Discarding Sabot
ARDE	Armament Research and Development Establishment
ATDU	Armour Trials Development Unit
BAOR	British Army of the Rhine
BATUS	British Army Training Unit Suffield
BV	Boiling Vessel
CVR(T)	Combat Vehicle Reconnaissance (Tracked)
FIPS	Fuel Injection Pump System
FMBT	Future Main Battle Tank
FVEE	Fighting Vehicle Engineering Establishment
FVRDE	Fighting Vehicles Research and Development Establishment
GPMG	General Purpose Machine Gun
GSFG	Group of Soviet Forces Germany
GSR	General Staff Requirement
HESH	High Explosive Squash Head
HVG	High Velocity Gun
IFCS	Improved Fire Control System
II	Image Intensifier
IR	Infra-red
MBSGD	Multi-Barrelled Smoke Grenade Discharger
MBT	Main Battle Tank
MRS	Muzzle Reference System
NBC	Nuclear Biological Chemical
OPFOR	Opposing Force
OTS	On Tank Stereo
RAC	Royal Armoured Corps – ie, RTR and Cavalry Regiments
REME	Royal Electrical and Mechanical Engineers
RCT	Royal Corps of Transport
RHA	Rolled Homgeneous Armour
RMG	Ranging Machine Gun
ROF	Royal Ordnance Factory
RTR	Royal Tank Regiment
SOXMIS	Soviet Mission
TISH	Thermal Imaging Seeker Head
TIT	Tank Infantry Telephone
TLS	Tank Laser Sight
TOGS	Thermal Observation and Gunnery System
UBRE	Unit Bulk Refuelling Equipment
VOR	Vehicle Off Road
WRCO	Wine Rack (Cavalry Officer)

Bibliography

User Handbook for Tank Combat 120 mm Chieftain Mk 1, 2 and 3 AC14908.

User Handbook for Tank Combat 120 mm Chieftain Mk 5 – 12 AC62259.

User Handbook Khalid 4030/2 MBT KHA 1030.

Preliminary production schedule Shir Iran 1 Issue 2 Feb 1977 MVEE.

Project 4030 Re-engining of Iranian Chieftains with CV 12 800 bhp Engine. MOD Procurement Executive.

Dunstan, Simon, *Chieftain MBT,* Osprey 2003.

Forty, George, *Chieftain,* Ian Allen 1979.

Griffin, Rob, *Chieftain,* Crowood 2001.

Hooton, E.R., Cooper, Tom, Nadimi, Farzin, *Middle East War No. 5 and 6,* Hellion and Company 2016.

Taylor, Dick, *Challenger 1 Owner's Workshop Manual,* Haynes Publishing 2015.

Taylor, Dick, *Chieftain MBT – Owner's Workshop Manual,* Haynes Publishing 2016.

Various documents from the National Archives at Kew – too numerous and boring to list here...

The Tank Museum Archive and Library – well worth a visit – they have no idea what a treasure trove they have!

Various *Tank Magazine* (RTR 1962–1996)

Fort Benning *Armor Magazine* Sept – Oct 1995. Major Robert A Nelson PB 17-95-5

Internet

TankNutDave.com

Wikipedia – (with caution)

Facebook – Chieftain Tank Appreciation Society